Farming for the Landless
new perspectives on the cultivation of our honeybee

To

Morgan & Rich

for the collection, love

Sarah.

sarah waring

Farming for the Landless
new perspectives on the cultivation of our honeybee

PLATIN

ℙLATIN

First published in Great Britain in 2015 by Platin Press

ISBN 978-0-9569404-6-9

www.farmingforthelandless.com

for
Christopher

in memory of
Alic

Cultivation

two

Protest. Toxic limits. Dust drift. The cheap fix.
Pressure from all sides: parasites, viruses and pesticides. Proof.
Lobbying and political fallout. The suspension.

51

Armin Trenkel
Agricultural scientist, Landwirtschaftliches Technologiezentrum
(Agricultural Technology Centre), Baden-Württemberg, Germany

56

Hemma Köglberger
Small-scale beekeeper and agricultural scientist,
Agentur für Gesundheit und Ernährungssicherheit
(Agency for Health and Food Security), Lower Austria, Austria

64

Adaptation

three
Domestic-feral. Swarming and proliferation.
Taking control: a docile and productive bee. A remote site.
Exporting a loss of distinction. Shipped in en-mass.
The hybrid pool. Losing control: genetic introgression.
Responsibility. Local rearing, the world over.
87

Bee-rearing station
Upper Carniola, Slovenia
93

Aleš Gregorc
Professor and researcher of honeybee rearing,
Agricultural Institute of Slovenia, Ljubljana, Slovenia
107

Adaptation

four

Far from cultivation. A place to thrive. Climate and change.
A place to survive. Co-adaptation. Choice intervention.
A considerate future.

115

Helen Bergqvist
Regional beekeeping expert, Lapland, Sweden
116

Conservation

five

Concrete honey. Dead nature and the 'life indicator'.
Up-close and hands-on. Bees as community. Quantifying forage.
Connecting habitat. Worth, value and use.
Conserving a farmed creature. All beekeepers.

135

Olivier Darné
Artist beekeeper, Parti Poétique, St. Denis, Paris, France
137

Caroline Birchall
Small-scale beekeeper, ecologist and Bee Collective founder,
London, UK
150

epilogue

introduction

The honeybee, *Apis mellifera*, is a species on the cusp of culture and nature. Whereas inside the hive it is evidently a kept creature adapted to its containment, foraging, swarming and mating flights are all reminders that the honeybee is principally an untamed, social insect responding to its colony's needs. With expansive colony sizes, proliferate reproduction and broad feeding habits, *Apis mellifera* is vigorous within its environment. Our cultural appreciation of the honeybee reflects the opportunistic ways we've found to benefit from this inherent productivity. Honey, the foodstuff made from nectar to feed colonies, is also a sweet and nutritious addition to our diet, often connoting a gift from nature that simply needs collecting. The practice of following bees and gathering honey can be dated back to Mesolithic times and yet we're obviously far removed from the hunter-gatherers of our past. Over time, we've become bee*keepers* by providing colonies with convenient shelter, utilising their innate behaviour to nest in dark cavities. Since at least 2,400 BC in Ancient Egypt, we've trialled and perfected methods of keeping bees for a more reliable honey harvest. By incrementally developing these careful methods to contain colonies without wholly disturbing their busy, beneficial behaviour, we've also encouraged an even more productive bee.

Managing hordes of insects involves much more than housing colonies to harvest their honey, however. The beekeeper's practice routinely involves regulating colony development, moving hives to habitats with plentiful forage, providing top-up food in leaner months and treating colonies against diseases. Many beekeepers also choose a subspecies or specific breed for their apiary, commonly selecting for high productivity combined with ease of maintenance. In many ways, keeping bees is comparable to other forms of husbandry. Farming dairy cattle, for example, includes similar aspects such as providing shelter, developing the herd, ensuring access to fodder, checking for ailments, as well as deciding on an appropriate breed; milk and honey are both managed harvests. Although bees, as foragers rather than grazers, cannot be totally confined, they are undeniably reared creatures. Under our care, the honeybee has become a form of livestock.

Despite this fact, beekeeping remains conceptually distinct from farming and is more often described as a hobby. In the popular imagination it's a genteel pursuit with a history of cloisters and private walled gardens. We picture an eccentrically dressed character in a white all-in-one suit among a model arrangement of secluded hives surrounded by cultivated flowers. The beekeeper is mysteriously involved in the prudent inspection of a buzzing mass with smoke and a mask, simultaneously protected from and enshrouded by this environment. We're intrigued by such an outlandish activity, and yet any hives we happen to spot dotted in the landscape remain unassuming. Although we know they conceal whole colonies, we may not associate the odd honeybee we see with those boxes. Each hive remains outwardly plain and static. As beekeepers with both large and small apiaries often keep their hives on wasteland, behind hedgerows and along field margins, most hives remain discreet within their surroundings. With no owner in sight, we're unlikely to imagine the occasional yet heavy labour necessary to move hives from place to place, to reposition them nearer plentiful, seasonal forage. Demarcation and permanence form a large part of our standard impression of agriculture: fields, gates, fences and hedges, the farmhouse, barns and yards. The established position of the farm in the landscape is representative of land ownership. The inconspicuous and portable apiary is modest in comparison, existing both physically and perceptually on the fringes of agriculture: beekeeping is farming for the landless.

Although unrecognised in standard agricultural classification, even when commercially undertaken, beekeeping is central to food production. When honeybees collect nectar and pollen to feed their colony, they simultaneously pollinate plants, many of which we grow as staple crops. Without honeybees, a wide variety of fruit, vegetables, cereals, seeds, nuts, oils, herbs, spices and medicinal plants wouldn't be systematically pollinated. As the honeybee repeatedly visits the same source of forage in its thousands, it is also a highly efficient worker; unsurprisingly, of all pollinating insects, this particular species has become our specialist in the field. Large-scale monocultural farming, which requires reliable and timely pollination, particularly benefits from the temporary location of many hives near a crop in flower. Whereas small-scale beekeepers might choose to relocate hives closer to plentiful forage, commercial beekeepers are specifically contracted to service these crops. Long rows of hives lining fields are indicative of a valuable trade: while plants are being pollinated, bees are collecting copious forage; the arable farmer expects a higher yield and the beekeeper more honey. Within this reciprocal arrangement adapted from nature, both the honeybee and the beekeeper are without doubt vital to modern farming practice.

Rather than thriving from this positive exchange, however, the honeybee is ailing, and its decline is occurring on a scale that cannot be ignored. Initial media interest focusing on disturbingly empty hives has been followed by articles, books and documentaries further raising public awareness, which in turn have led to a series of high-profile campaigns, petitions and even political fallout across Europe. We've been warned that our mutually beneficial relationship with the honeybee, and with it our own well-being, is under threat. We've related one-third of the food we eat with the work of the honeybee and firmly associated its demise with potential crop failure; the economic risk of losing a reliable means of crop pollination has been calculated in billions per year in the UK alone. While reporting has been sensational, current honeybee losses are alarming and the problems we face very real.

Within a short period of time the honeybee has become indicative of environmental discord, raising pertinent questions about the state of modern agriculture. Beekeeping has become much more than a classic pastime now that this ancient work has acquired new contexts. As the bee we keep bridges the gap between farming and the environment, it provides an ideal opportunity to develop discourse regarding contemporary land use. The farmed bee, our honeybee, has become a matter of compound ecological and cultural significance.

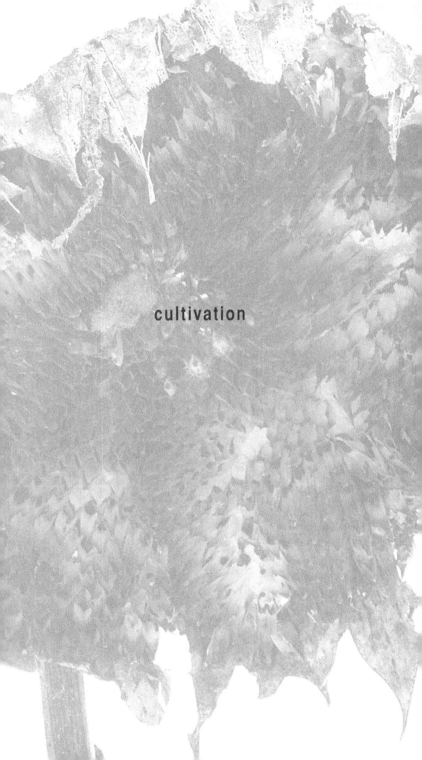

cultivation

one

In spring, as winter's chill passes, beekeepers ardently watch their hives for signs of life. Having left their bees to their own devices, they won't have seen inside the hive for several months; each colony, actively keeping warm in a cluster, has remained undisturbed to give it the best chance of survival. The first worker bees to emerge, testing the air beyond the hive and looking for early blooms, are always a promising sight. If a hive shows little action, the beekeeper may well have lost the colony, and this has become an increasingly common occurrence. To find 10% fewer colonies in an apiary after the hard winter months wouldn't be considered unusual, but since 2007 losses of 50–75% have been frequently recorded.[1]* Worse and stranger still, while winter was once the only vulnerable time of the beekeeping calendar, many now experience colony losses during the foraging season when colonies ought to be at their most vigorous. Such disasters understandably instil anxiety and are regarded with great suspicion. News stories more reminiscent of science fiction or murder mystery than natural history have reported whole colony disappearances where bees up and leave their hives en-mass overnight. In certain cases, bees abandon their honey stores, which even more bizarrely remain untouched by neighbouring colonies ordinarily known to rob empty hives.

* In the UK, for example, beekeepers in the south-east in particular incurred extreme losses from 2007–8, as exampled by the then chairman of the London Beekeepers Association, John Chapman, who lost 30 out of 40 hives. Other associations in nearby regions experienced similar critical situations: the Harrow Beekeepers Association lost 50% of hives and the Pinner and Ruislip Beekeepers Association 75%.

Recent honeybee losses have often been referred to as 'Colony Collapse Disorder', a term originally coined in the US. A thorough account of the disorder, outlined in *Guardian* journalist Alison Benjamin and co-writer Brian McCallum's book *A World Without Bees* (2008), attributes the first instance of CCD to a commercial Florida beekeeper who, during November 2006, found 360 out of 400 colonies devoid of worker bees. A 90% decrease over a couple of weeks is a devastating loss, and so the beekeeper contacted an official Pennsylvanian State inspector. Scientists at the local University and Pennsylvania and Florida's departments of agriculture then investigated the few dead worker bees found in the abandoned hives and identified "many abnormalities, including scarring on the digestive tract, swollen kidneys and evidence of a fungal or yeast infection in the sting gland."[2] They called the clinical signs they found 'Fall Dwindle Disease'.

By the beginning of the following year, what may have appeared to some as bad practice on the part of one beekeeper became harder to dismiss as many more reported similar losses. A group of scientists from the Agricultural Research Service at the United States Department of Agriculture and a Penn State University entomologist reviewed the case. Within the space of just three months, what had initially been identified as a restrained 'dwindle' of colonies in autumn was reclassified as a more instantaneous and violent 'collapse'. Clinical signs, originally identified as a 'disease', had morphed into a 'disorder'.

At the time, entomologists already knew of many factors negatively affecting bee health but had no single answer to the cause of accelerated bee deaths. A combination of environmental and biological conditions affecting colony health can be readily accommodated within the notion of a disorder and a new name with gravitas was perhaps the ideal means to focus attention on a diverse range of concerns. Research with limited funding benefited from heightened media coverage, which raised public awareness and encouraged more immediate government investment. As information and influence often travels rapidly via media channels across the Atlantic, CCD soon became the label for honeybee maladies in the UK as well.

This isn't the first time that a term has been broadly applied to describe potentially different circumstances regarding bee health. Historically, as Benjamin and McCallum state:

> From the so-called Isle of Wight Disease ... through to Disappearing Disease in the States in the 1970s and now Colony Collapse Disorder at the beginning of the 21st century, periodic bee calamities have often been lumped together when each outbreak could be due to entirely different factors.[3]

In the case of the 'Isle of Wight Disease', an initially very localised disease soon became a national phenomenon. UK scientists Peter Neumann and Norman Carreck when commenting in 2010 on contemporary honeybee colony losses also recognised parallels with this precedent:

> Almost exactly a century ago, in 1906, beekeepers on the Isle of Wight, a small island off the south coast of England, noticed that many of their honeybee colonies were dying, with numerous bees crawling from the hive, unable to fly. Despite some sceptical beekeepers suggesting that this was 'paralysis', a condition which had long been known, the colony losses were widely reported in the media, and beekeepers became convinced that the cause was a novel and highly infectious disease, and the condition was soon reported from all parts of Britain. Within a few years, all losses of bees in Britain, from whatever cause, were ascribed to 'Isle of Wight Disease'.[4]

The assertion of an indiscriminate colony disease led to several incorrect identifications of its cause. After significant speculation over the Isle of Wight Disease, one culprit in particular became widely accepted. In 1919, Dr J. Rennie observed a previously unknown parasite and published a paper in 1921[5] identifying *Acarapis woodii*, a tracheal mite that feeds internally on the honeybee's haemolymph.* As a result, the Isle of Wight Disease was renamed 'Acarine Disease' despite counter-indicative results lurking in the scientist's original experiments. Evidence of honeybees flying even though heavily infested with mites or crawling whilst uninfected by the parasite didn't detract from *Acarapis woodii* being commonly considered the root cause for decades to come. It's tempting to speculate why it might have been admissible, especially after WWI, to resolutely identify and isolate a distinct invading enemy. Increasing doubt was cast on *Acarapis woodii* being the sole cause of this debilitating disease, however, when beekeepers, who couldn't remove the parasite easily, found that some colonies survived this early blight period with the mite. Nevertheless, it was not until 1963, following significant advances in microscope technology, that bee pathologist Leslie Bailey was able to identify what had actually wiped out so many colonies at the beginning of the century.[6]† Bailey's research ascertained that honeybee decline at the time had been caused by something even less discernible: 'Chronic Bee Paralysis Virus', a viral infection in bees that remains latent unless triggered by external factors. Bailey asserted that a combination of factors were at the root of the problem, including environmental circumstances. On the Isle of Wight in 1906, an exceptionally hot April was followed by sub-zero temperatures in May which confined large springtime colonies to their hives for longer periods of time than is usual or healthy.

* the equivalent of blood in invertebrates
† Bailey published variously on the subject, but his first report appeared after a lecture given to the Central Association of Beekeepers on 13th March 1963.

A virus triggered by a parasite was exacerbated by climatic irregularity which in combination led to the death of many colonies. Although there could have been no way of knowing a virus was at the root of a disease in the first instance of the Isle of Wight Disease, it's worth gleaning some wisdom from these events. When various symptoms are corralled under one guise, poor assumptions are likely to be made about their causes; although there may be advantages to using an influential name such as CCD as a 'catch all' to generate interest, it's unlikely to lead to practical solutions.

As CCD's influence is wider than the Isle of Wight or Acarine Disease was a century ago,* our contemporary disorder may be masking even greater discrepancies of cause and effect over extensive physical distance. It may be that honeybee deaths in Europe and the US are related but different environmental conditions prevent their direct comparison. Equally, the scale of beekeeping practices is very different in the US to the UK. Over an entire continent, there's ample climatic difference to extend the honeybee's foraging season beyond its natural scope by transporting hives from one side of the US to another. Although hives are also transported in the UK, there's simply not the equivalent geographical stretch that would provide the economies of scale for larger beekeeping operations. Articulated lorries transporting hundreds of beehives long distances between crops can only exist in the imagination on the European side of the Atlantic. Benjamin and McCallum quantify the immense scale of US commercial beekeeping by stating:

> It could be argued that the expansion of California's almond industry from 90,000 acres in the 1950s to more than six times that by 2008 is the single most important event in US beekeeping in the past 60 years

* Although the Isle of Wight Disease was considered a relatively localised problem, it's worth noting that the USA enforced the 1922 Honeybee Act in order to restrict honeybee colony imports from Europe in response to UK colony losses.

> … Half of all the honeybees in the United States have
> to be trucked into Central Valley during February.
> Around 3,000 trucks make the journey from as far
> as Florida, each carrying some 480 beehives stacked
> four high. In the cool hours before sunrise more than
> one million colonies of bees are unloaded between the
> endless rows of almond trees.[7]

The Californian almond, covering approximately 540,000 acres of land, is a prime example of intensive monoculture which has become highly-demanding to pollinate. In order to produce the highest almond yield possible, huge, disproportionate numbers of colonies are located near flowering trees. As a result, competition for forage is high and, as almond flowers produce little nectar, beekeepers need to provide colonies with supplementary food* at this time. The rigours of almond pollination in the US also impact further hive transportation to locations that do provide the necessary quantities of forage for colonies to feed from. This is a major undertaking if you keep 70,000 hives, as the largest apiary in the US during Benjamin and McCallum's research did. In comparison, the largest apiary in the UK contains around 2,000 hives and represents a much more moderate and manageable operation.†

In fact, only 40 hives are required for an apiary to be officially considered commercial in the UK. Government statistics attempting to identify the scope of UK beekeeping – such as those published in the 2011 document from Northern Ireland's Department of Agricultural and Rural Development (DARD)[8] – list over 40,000 beekeepers working across Northern Ireland, Scotland, England and

---

* Beekeepers occasionally feed colonies a dilute syrup of sugar and water, and other sugary compounds to supplement sources of forage or replace harvested honey.

† Chain Bridge Honey Farm, located near Berwick-upon-Tweed, is a good example of a large-scale operation in the UK with around 2,000 hives, which nevertheless only transports colonies within a 40-mile radius.

Wales that collectively registered around 271,600 hives. Interestingly, the majority of beekeepers detailed in this report maintained apiaries containing fewer than forty hives: UK beekeepers listed an average 7–8 colonies in Scotland, 5–6 in England and Wales, and as few as 3–5 in Northern Ireland. Beekeeping is practised on such a small-scale in the UK that more than 99% of practitioners are officially classified as 'hobbyists'. Given such a broad statistic, what better way to elucidate meaning from categorisation than to meet a beekeeper with a few hives at the bottom of the garden?

Edwin Clark
Hobbyist beekeeper, Lincolnshire, UK

The first time I see Edwin Clark is an impromptu moment: he's halfway up a ladder and a tree passing down instructions, and it's clear that there's not a moment to lose. This is a tentative yet purposeful act. It's one of those rare occasions when a skilled beekeeper attempts to capture a honeybee swarm looking for a new place to nest, and it looks dangerous. I'm witness to this unusual event at a safe distance in London though, watching a video clip shot by Edwin's son Richard, a colleague of mine. In a flurry of frenetic movement onscreen, I'm catching my first glimpse of a swarm in action until, that is, the footage stops, abruptly. I sit back in my chair to imagine fields of apple trees and conjure the moment after the recording finished when the bees would have been collected. Although short, this incidental movie has left a lasting impression.

* * *

No sooner do I arrive at Edwin's house in a small Lincolnshire village than I'm being invited to inspect his colonies. Immediately I feel both excited and apprehensive at the chance to step beyond the pages of news reports and journal articles into the realm of living bees. Without pause for further thought, my everyday city clothes are transformed into an all-in-one suit, hood and gloves, and any minor concerns of appearance are abandoned to the practicality of what I'm wearing.

Edwin then rolls up some corrugated card into a smoker, and as soon as it's lit we're ready. The smoker is going to simulate a fire to the bees: rather than protecting themselves against human intruders, they'll instinctively eat honey to prepare themselves for a potential hive evacuation. I, meanwhile, will have to work against my instinct to panic and run from bees buzzing around me. From early childhood, although fascinated, I've had an aversion to birds and insects in flight, and am not sure how I'll react to being surrounded. These bees are no pets, regardless of their domestic surroundings.

Making bee talk with Edwin is proving an educational as well as calming antidote to my fears, however. It's a fine, sunny morning, the garden is brimming with daffodil blooms and, despite the relatively early hour, worker bees are already busy foraging for their colonies and aren't nearly as interested in me as I am in them. First, we slide out and inspect a white tray from underneath each hive. Edwin is looking for telltale signs of *Varroa destructor*, the bright orange mite that lives on honeybees as a parasite and is large enough to spot by eye. Apart from a few deceptive balls of pollen, the trays are clean and Edwin seems satisfied to move on to opening up one of the hives. As I step back, all that is initially revealed is a bag of 'candy', a sweet fondant used as a top-up feed for bees in leaner months. Several bees are working around the top of the hive, but with no extra levels, known as 'supers', to extend the honey-building sections of the hive, there's little to see here so early in the season. Edwin then removes the 'queen excluder', a layer of narrow metal strips that only workers can pass through, and immediately the buzzing of the hive is amplified; my experience becomes more saturated than colour photographs of bees taken at rest on summer flowers. Although I'm increasingly aware of more bees around me, I concentrate on Edwin who's inspecting frames from the hive. He's looking for the colony's queen, who, despite her larger size, is proving difficult to trace. Depending on points of view, the queen is either considered the head of a colony or the most managed member of a group: although the sole egg layer, the queen is dependent on worker bees for food and it's the workers, rather than the queen, that prepare the colony for her to swarm. As another frame is produced from the hive, I notice a rounded cocoon on its edge and point it out to Edwin. A colony preparing to replace its queen produces virgin queen cups by extending standard cells and increasing the feed of otherwise regular worker bee larvae. This might be a new queen in the making, and so Edwin swiftly removes the cocoon to maintain the stability of the colony. He knows that his elusive queen is definitely in there somewhere and is going to try to ensure she stays that way.

Once satisfied with his inspection, Edwin asks if I'd like to handle a frame and, after the briefest moment that seems to make its own decision, I'm suddenly holding one of the busiest frames clutched at arms length between my rigid, gloved hands. While I carefully rotate the frame in mid-air, Edwin discusses how he might move these hives mid-season. He's considering taking advantage of the abundant crops nearby and moving his bees closer to the oilseed rape fields that ought to accelerate their honey production. The bees on the frame I'm holding haven't stopped their communication and work: one bee is cleaning its antennae, another worker is calmly walking over others, bees are rubbing their pollen-laden legs. Surely this colony wouldn't mind being moved a few miles closer to readily available forage?

The apple orchards in my mind's eye have transformed and materialised into regimented, homogenised fields, however. In the UK, we now grow almost five times as much oilseed rape as we do fruit and vegetables* and orchards cover only 3.2% of the equivalent land amassed to oilseed rape.[9] The time when farmers may have listed a few hives as an integral part of their livestock to pollinate crops and produce honey has seemingly long passed. Over the past 50–60 years in particular, the aim of increasing productivity within a competitive

---

*In 2012, oilseed rape was grown in 3,142,000 hectares while fruit and vegetables combined amassed only 157,000 hectares. Although oilseed rape can be harvested to produce vegetable cooking oil and is being developed as bio-fuel, if sown excessively, it's especially prone to disease and crop failure.

market has changed the face of much UK agriculture; many farms have closed and land that has been subsumed into much larger operations is now being used for intensive farming. Crops grown for bulk harvests rather than food variety dominate most arable and horticultural fields. The accessibility of land in Lincolnshire in particular has left it open to intensive farming practices and the development of major operations with minimal crop diversity is now commonplace. From behind the mesh of my protective face mask, looking at Edwin as one eccentrically dressed character to another, I begin to sense the disparity between the scale of his practice and that of the surrounding farmland. Having been so readily welcomed into the world of beekeeping and captivated by the colony, I could see that the bees weren't going to be my greatest confrontation after all; the disquiet I was now feeling emanated directly from the bright yellow fields beyond.

—

Although Edwin doesn't profit financially from the pollination his bees perform locally, the proximity of his colonies to commercial crops undoubtedly benefits arable farmers. In total, the practices of around 39,670 small-scale beekeepers throughout the UK intrinsically and yet unofficially support fresh food production. Government departments overseeing agriculture and rural environments acknowledge that bees contribute enormously to the economic value of harvests, suggesting that "the crop pollination provided by bees in Britain and the north of Ireland is estimated to be worth between £120–£200 million",[10] and yet they rarely include beekeeping in literature detailing UK agricultural practices. Instead, standard reports prioritise the output of pastoral, arable and horticultural farming with figures focusing on animal numbers and harvest quantities. Given the small number of hives in UK apiaries on average, officials who look at beekeeping harvests also find little to report. UK honey production returns minimal if any profit, averaging annual revenue of around £45.50 per hive.[11]

Some beekeepers like Edwin therefore only produce honey for personal consumption. Commonly, small-scale UK beekeepers do not expect financially profitable harvests.

Classifying most UK beekeepers as hobbyists might be misleading considering their role in pollination but there's something unifying in this description, as apiculture, for many, is a part-time activity quite aside from a career. Successfully managing the behaviour of masses of stinging insects requires more than the hobbyist's enthusiasm, however. Beekeepers have methodical approaches that need to be learnt through study as well as hands-on husbandry. Edwin, for example, may only keep a few colonies but his practice should be recognised as much more than an amateur pursuit. His extensive beekeeping experience – accumulated from agricultural training at eighteen through to retirement – is shared via a regional beekeeping association through talks with groups of aspiring beekeepers and, importantly, as a National Swarm Co-ordinator on call to retrieve bees. Beekeeping is a skilled practice ideally acquired through the guidance of an expert. Although Edwin may not consider himself a farmer any more than the government classify him as a professional beekeeper, his practice without doubt contributes to a rich history of husbandry in the UK. Is it not then too simplistic to categorise the collective expertise of beekeepers primarily on the amount of hives they own or the amount of profit they return from honey harvests?

Equally, of the less than 1% that *do* manage 40 hives or more and harvest their honey for profit, why are these beekeepers also unacknowledged within standard farming categorisation? While there may be few commercial beekeepers in Great Britain and Northern Ireland – no more than 330 registered in 2010[12] – as an average based on hive numbers, one in every four to five honeybees we see foraging could be reared by one of these professionals. This is a significant amount of livestock. In Scotland, although there are only 30 beekeeping businesses registered, they collectively run

25% of British commercial hives. Large apiaries contain around 1,000–1,250 hives[13] and parallel the scale of specialist soft fruit production that has developed to cover 4,075 acres of land around the east coast of Scotland since 2007.[14] Raspberries, blackberries and blackcurrants are well established to suitably mild and wet Scottish summers, but to maximise yields and extend the growing seasons 70% of these fruits are grown under polythene.[15] Wild bees that would ordinarily visit raspberry canes can't pollinate covered crops so readily, of course, and so kept bees are useful on these farms. While honeybees are the workers of choice, it's telling that in some instances bumblebees are being used in the same way despite their inability to produce honey.* One clear aim of the commercial beekeeper is to provide a guaranteed pollination service to those farmers who would otherwise risk less reliable results.

For UK commercial beekeepers, although pollination services may provide their main income, annual contracts with other farmers rarely provide enough profit for businesses to thrive. Unlike in the US where pollination contracts merit extensive mobile apiaries, equivalent UK businesses tend to supplement their income with other enterprises. It's common, for example, to find specialist honey from UK commercial beekeepers for sale in farmers' markets and other local outlets: beekeepers with commercial apiaries move their colonies not only to pollinate agricultural crops but also to position hives near sources of the most flavoursome honey forage. While few beekeepers would ever try and market pure oilseed rape honey,† there are many honeys

---

* Farmed bumble bees would no doubt have proved particularly viable during the period of excessively poor honeybee health in Scotland from 2007–2010 when colonies suffered from above average European Foul Brood and American Foul Brood, which are caused by highly-contagious bacteria that infect honeybee larvae.

† Oilseed rape produces a light, mild honey that crystallises quickly and is therefore generally used as an ingredient for processed food or blended honey.

available that aren't affiliated with commercial crops, such as chestnut or acacia, which dictate the location of colonies in places away from agricultural land at specific times of the foraging season. The increasing scale of arable and horticultural business in the UK may have encouraged some beekeepers to extend their practices to meet pollination demands, but bees need sufficient sources of forage throughout the season and not just at the zenith of crops in bloom. Giving colonies an abundant source of nectar and pollen at an intense, developmental part of the foraging season will encourage larger colonies that subsequently need feeding all the more. Commercial beekeepers not only move their hives regularly to pollinate crops and produce specialist honey but also to adequately feed their colonies. There are few locations in the UK where there's enough space or year-round forage to keep large apiaries together and so commercial beekeepers tend to place their hives on different sites, especially at the tail end of the season when forage is scarce. Those beekeepers who've developed their apiaries from the small to relatively large-scale do so within a compact landmass, limited climatic variation and in relation to increasingly simplified crop and habitat diversity.

Mike Thurlow

Commercial beekeeper, Orchid Apiaries, Norfolk, UK

I turn a corner within the concrete of London's Southbank Centre and a medley of aromas, sights and sounds suddenly enliven my senses. The first sign reads '*slow*-roast hog sandwiches' and I know I've found the right place. Speciality meat and cheeses, fresh veg and homemade preserves all tempt me to wander the aisles of brightly illuminated and colourful market stalls while I seek out the 'Slow Food' information tent; I'm after more detail about the not-for-profit organisation that promotes an alternative to the usual conveniences of inner city food retail. Once at the info tent, it's not long before I'm talking to the market's organiser about my research, and no sooner do I mention beekeeping than we're off in search of Mike Thurlow. From a distance I notice his stall with its gold-topped glass jars and, as we approach, the person standing quietly behind rows of delicately balanced honey stacks, candles and honeybee trinkets animates. Mike's warmth evidently comes from discussing apiculture rather than the late season and, given my own affinity for bee knowledge, I soon become his next willing audience.

With his distinctive east-country accent, Mike begins by discussing the extent of his practice. Orchid Apiaries, based near the River Yare outside Norwich in Norfolk, is a medium-sized business that mixes the static positioning of hives at 20 or so sites across the county with hive transportation for pollination services beyond Norfolk. Mike's bees can be working the flowering willow and sycamore trees of Norfolk at the beginning of the spring in April, before being moved to commercial fruit orchards in Kent or mass borage fields in the Yorkshire Wolds, and ending up back in Norfolk for the flowering ivy by the end of summer into autumn. The breadth of Mike's choice of locations is telling. As a commercial beekeeper, one of his main incomes comes from the pollination of agricultural crops, but he's determined to also give his bees the benefits of foraging locations where local plant diversity can be found in rural Norfolk. The range of honey on sale from this single beekeeper is impressive, from individual crop honey, including heather and lime, to that named by its source location such as Wherryman's honey from the Wherryman's Way in the Yare Valley or that produced at a regeneration site on Cranwich Heath. This is a commercial beekeeper whose concern for the environment and the health of his livestock leads him to actively support local environmental projects that aim to return diversity to rural areas.

Mike's activity is determined more and more by the changing Norfolk countryside. Staple foraging sites of fruit orchards and flowering hedgerows have made way for larger fields of barley and sugar beet of no use to bees. Traditional orchards, once prominent throughout England, have declined by 63% since 1950 and now cover less than 400 hectares in Norfolk.[16] Mike's colonies therefore need to be trucked further than in the past; he has necessarily become as dependent on other commercial farmers for forage as they are on him for pollination. Despite this reliance, Mike has some curt words to say about other farmers, suggesting that not even his fellow stallholders are necessarily aware of how important the work he and his colonies do is for their businesses.

Mike's vocal opinion has already led to his inclusion in a documentary. First televised on BBC4 in 2009, *Who Killed the Honeybee?* charts the recent discourse about pollination and bee health. Shot predominantly in sunny California, the contrasting footage recorded across a wet winter's day in Norfolk initially places Mike with a few hives in tall, dormant grass surrounded by desaturated nursery beech trees lining a dark turned field. The scale of Mike's apiary, despite being commercial, clearly distinguishes this beekeeper's practice from his counterpart's in the US. Posed beside his well-used Land Rover and dressed appropriately in a sturdy raincoat, Mike explains his experience of bee losses since 2002. He describes "bucketfuls of dead bees … hundreds of thousands of dead bees"[17] and the repercussions of this mysterious mass decline:

> If it's one of the recognised diseases then you know what it is and hopefully you can take some action. In this scenario, you have no recourse to do anything: absolutely zilch. You've just got to stand by and watch them die and when it's your livelihood that's pretty tough.[18]

Framed against a red brick fireplace in his home a few scenes later, Mike recounts one winter in particular:

We had one load of bees that came back from
pollination that had all been together from April
going back to October. When they came back from
pollination, they were split three ways: one third
went into a wood — 200 acres predominantly of
lime trees — and no bees died there at all, and on
the other two sites — intensive agricultural areas
— that's where the colonies collapsed. Something
triggered the bees to collapse on those two sites.
It must be connected with the agricultural crops:
the sprays and the seed treatments. There's no
other explanation.[19]

This, Mike's most incisive comment of the interview, is
accompanied by his slight caustic laughter, part incredulous, part
insistent. When I ask Mike about his perception of the scale of
poor honeybee health in the UK, he says that it's probably even
worse than the statistics suggest. Official figures, in Mike's
opinion, can't be accurate because not all beekeepers admit to
inspectors that their colonies are suffering. Many he knows
personally are worried that their losses would be considered
malpractice or unprofessional. Commercial beekeepers often
rely on the revenue they gain from large-scale pollination and
it's perhaps bad for business to admit that you may not have the
bees needed to fulfil contracts. In the short term, some decide
to repopulate their hives as quickly as possible and carry on
regardless: business as usual. To conceal bee deaths locks the
commercial beekeeper into a negative cycle, however. If they don't
assert the scale of the problem in the first instance, they have
little scope to voice concern or gain compensation later. More
importantly, if, as Mike believes, honeybees are struggling within
the farming practices they service, beekeepers may not find it
easy to address the problem directly. Although honeybees collect
forage while pollinating, they do so as a secondary aspect of a

commercial exchange intended to provide assured crops. Arable and horticultural farmers who pay for pollination aren't therefore expected to provide any reassurance to beekeepers. They're only dependent on bee farmers at one vital time of the year and, in economic terms, are the customers of a service.

I'm left wondering about the situation in which Mike and other beekeepers like him find themselves. They know their work is invaluable, but they're not well supported within the hierarchy of contemporary farming practices. A commercial beekeeper may appear inconspicuous within a Slow Food market — honey is after all the ultimate slow food — but few UK beekeepers, especially commercial practitioners, can escape the influence of the industrial food chain. There's no doubt that Mike's personal ethics support a more ecologically sound environment, but it's near impossible for any beekeeper to protect their bees day-to-day from agricultural chemicals in the field.

—

The sprays and seed treatments that concern beekeepers like Mike are forms of pesticide known as plant protection products. Available as insecticides, fungicides and herbicides, these products are collectively aimed at maximising yield by combating crop feeding insects, diseases and weeds. Although based on naturally occurring toxins, modern pesticides are synthetic products far removed from original plant and mineral sources such as dried chrysanthemum flowers and tobacco extracts. During the late 1930s and 1940s, formulas appropriated from WWII chemical warfare were used to intensify pesticide production. The chemical industry has since developed further technological means to produce synthetic compounds with even more concentrated toxicity. Pesticides have therefore become all the more readily available, affordable and profitable. Classes of agricultural chemicals now exist within an array of products from bacterium repellent to bird deterrents and, despite their relative infancy, the spectrum and use of synthetic pesticides has burgeoned to the point that they're perceived not only as conventional but also conservative within general farming practices. In its current literature, the European Crop Protection Association states:

> Since farming began, pests and diseases have been a farmer's nightmare, destroying crops, poisoning food or making it inedible. In fact, there would be close to no agriculture without pest control. Farmers also have little to no control over the climate, or the soil and the geographic environment in which the crops are grown. However one element they can control is the pests and diseases that destroy or damage crops.[20]

For those with a vested interest in pesticide production, the "farmer's nightmare" is wrought by nature's demons. Nature is perceived as the adversary of food production as opposed to its provider. The arguable lack of control the pro-pesticide lobby suggest we have over climate, soil and geography appears to present the ideal justification to throw all our force against troublesome pests. However, in our bid to eradicate certain insects, fungi and weeds, we indiscriminately affect other life. Pollinators are of course also insects and, as honeybees pollinate a broad range of plants commonly treated with pesticides, beekeepers are understandably worried that one farmer's plant protection has become another's poison.

Within their short history, various classes of synthetic pesticides have already been produced, widely distributed, proven overtly poisonous and consequently discontinued from common use. The seminal book by American marine biologist Rachel Carson, *Silent Spring* (1962), which provided convincing and popular argument to suspend many agricultural and garden plant protection products in the US, is lasting testament to the effects of chemical misuse. The following quote details one of several decisive moments that Carson chronicles as example to the US of pesticides under debate in Europe after many wild and game birds died in the UK:

> In England the major problem seems to be a specialised one, linked with the growing practice of treating seed with insecticides ... In the spring of 1960 a deluge of reports of dead birds reached British wildlife authorities, including the British Trust for Ornithology, the Royal Society for the Protection of Birds, and the Game Birds Association.
>
> *The place is like a battlefield [a landowner of Norfolk wrote]. My keeper has found innumerable corpses, including masses of small birds — chaffinches, greenfinches, linnets, hedge sparrows, also house sparrows ... the destruction of wildlife is quite pitiful. [A game keeper wrote]: My partridges have been wiped out with the dressed corn, also some pheasants and all other birds, hundreds of birds have been killed ... As a lifelong gamekeeper it has been a distressing experience for me. It is bad to see pairs of partridges that have died together.*
>
> ... A new wave of poisoning set in the following year. The death of 600 birds on a single estate in Norfolk was reported to the House of Lords and 100 pheasants died on a farm in North Essex. It soon became evident that more counties were involved than in 1960 (34 compared with 23). Lincolnshire, heavily agricultural, seemed to have suffered most, with reports of 10,000 birds dead. But destruction involved all of agricultural Britain,

from Angus in the north to Cornwall in the south,
from Anglesey in the west to Norfolk in the east.[21]

That very same year, a House of Commons special committee requested testimonials from agricultural and wildlife representatives in order to form a hearing, which as Carson further reports:

> ... convinced the committee that the threat to wildlife was 'most alarming'; it accordingly recommended to the House of Commons that:
>
> *the Minister of Agriculture and the Secretary of State for Scotland should secure the immediate prohibition for the use as seed dressings of compounds containing dieldrin, aldrin, or heptachlor, or chemicals of comparable toxicity.*
>
> The committee also recommended more adequate controls to ensure that chemicals were adequately tested under field as well as laboratory conditions before being put on the market.[22]

The UK government's caution regarding these pesticides was based on stark evidence. Birds, so often symbols of freedom, having died suddenly and in significant numbers, had made it impossible to ignore such disastrous and visible environmental impact; "pairs of partridges that have died together" are after all far more anthropomorphic than "bucketfuls of dead bees". In killing game birds, as well as wild birds, pesticides hadn't escaped the attention of influential landowners either. Agriculture had in this case not only contravened nature, it had inadvertently crossed its own line.

The recommendation that called for tighter controls on testing chemicals such as aldrin, dieldrin and heptachlor suggested that field as well as laboratory tests should be undertaken *prior* to use, which Carson considered "worth emphasising, is one of the great blank spots in pesticide research everywhere."[23] This point has consequently proven particularly prudent, as all three of these organochlorines are now known to be toxic to humans. Although some of the long-term effects of organochlorines are still being discovered, we now have additional evidence of the broad impacts of this chemical class, as summarised by environmental scientist Tim Flannery in *Here on Earth* (2010):

> Organochlorines take a very long time to degrade, which means that once they're out of the bottle they'll be around for years. They are also volatile, readily entering the atmosphere, and so spread far and wide. Because they cannot be dissolved in water yet dissolve easily in fat, once they are taken into a living body they tend to stay there, accumulating in fatty tissues such as the brain and reproductive organs.[24]

The fact that organochlorines steadily accumulate and magnify as they make their way up the food chain means that our use of these pesticides is overtly self-destructive. Although not restricted or banned in the EU until the early 1980s,* organochlorines were commonly replaced by organophosphates, which were considered a less obdurate class of chemicals. As Flannery further states, however, organophosphates have predictably proven to present their own problems:

> Compared with the obdurate organochlorines, they [organophosphates] have the virtue of breaking down relatively swiftly. Yet they are far more toxic

* As example, aldrin, the highly persistent organochlorine that readily breaks down in the body to form dieldrin, was restricted in 1981 and banned in 1991. Dieldrin, also produced and marketed independently of aldrin, was banned in 1981. Heptachlor, meanwhile, was banned in 1984.

> than the organochlorines — minute amounts can
> cause death ... Because the toxins spread swiftly
> and are cumulative, not a single ecosystem escaped
> their influence, with waterways being particularly
> vulnerable. Streams in more industrialised areas
> were ... entirely emptied of fish and other life.[25]

Extreme environmental destruction bartered against lower human toxicity shouldn't disguise the fact that even organophosphates have proven capable of reaching our food supplies, however. In another example from the UK, Carson reports early evidence in 1953 of an organophosphate nerve agent poisoning food:

> In England someone wondered what happened
> when bees made use of nectar from plants treated
> with systemics ... The result, as might have been
> predicted, was that the honey made by the bees
> also was contaminated with Schradan.[26]

In this case, an organophosphate had been transmitted from plant to honey via the bee's ordinarily beneficial activity; time and again, evidence suggests that no aspect of pesticide use, whether organophosphate or organochlorine-based, should realistically be considered in isolation.

Schradan may no longer be in use* but the same method of pesticide dispersal is still widely practiced. Systemic pesticides, which are readily available as sprays, soil treatments and seed coatings, work by permeating all parts of a plant as it grows; any chemical, regardless of its classification, can be produced as a systemic if it can be transmitted through a plant's vascular system. The very first systemic pesticide developed during the 1920s in the

* Schradan, a trade name pesticide containing active ingredient octamethylpyrophosphoramide, was withdrawn from production in 1964.

US, for example, was based on selenium, the element that occurs naturally yet sparingly in rocks and soil. It was formulated after the observation that sodium selenate rich wheat fields detract aphids and spider mites, but the systemic version of selenium passed highly-toxic residues to food as well as to crop-feeding insects and was soon discontinued as an agricultural pesticide. As Carson expressively characterises, our use of systemics creates a distinctly pervasive, alternate natural environment:

> The world of systemic insecticides is a weird world, surpassing the imaginings of the brothers Grimm — perhaps most closely akin to the cartoon world of Charles Addams. It is a world where the enchanted forest of the fairy-tales has become the poisonous forest in which an insect that chews a leaf or sucks the sap of a plant is doomed. It is a world where a flea bites a dog, and dies because the dog's blood has been made poisonous, where an insect may die from vapours emanating from a plant it has never touched, where a bee may carry poisonous nectar back to its hive and presently produce poisonous honey.[27]

The forcible language of an earlier protest may read more emotionally than we're currently used to but the focus of Carson's debate is still raging.

Yet another chemical class of pesticides commonly used as a systemic has since proven contentious for bees and beekeeping. Neonicotinoids, based on the well-known tobacco plant compound, nicotine – in use as a pesticide since the late 17th century – are extremely synthesised pesticides that bear little relationship to natural sources. Produced at high intensity and yet low density, neonicotinoids are considered non-toxic to humans and therefore have become readily authorised for many crop protection uses. Since their introduction in the 1990s, neonicotinoids have become one of the most highly-used chemical classes on arable and horticultural crops such as oilseed rape, corn and sunflower. When beekeepers like Mike Thurlow began finding honeybees dead from hives located near neonicotinoid-treated farmland, they had to ask if neonicotinoids were the cause. Would neonicotinoids prove to be as unexpectedly toxic as previous pesticides?

A dust drift forming over European fields and meadows has failed to settle without question. Recent incidences of acute honeybee losses, the earliest of which occurred in 1994 across France, have resulted in beekeepers rallying together in protest. French beekeepers, who suspected a newly introduced agricultural pesticide to be the cause, held public demonstrations that led to campaigning and, in due course, to legal action. The pesticide was imidacloprid, the neonicotinoid first sold throughout France as a systemic treatment on sunflower seeds under the Bayer CropScience trade name Gaucho. The bold, yellow flower that follows the sun – synonymous with optimism, prosperity, fecundity and ordinarily an attractive source of nectar and pollen to bees – had seemingly been distorted by the addition of this new chemical. Whereas beekeepers, especially those with commercial enterprises, had benefited enormously from large-scale sunflower production in the past, they were suddenly experiencing the opposite, as outlined in the thorough 2012 report of imidacloprid use as a systemic seed dressing in France by Laura Maxim and Jeroen van der Sluijs for the European Environment Agency:

> In affected apiaries, most hives were impacted. Those apiaries suffered a 40–70% loss in sunflower honey yield in the years after 1994, relative to the average yield obtained in previous years. Before 1994, the annual yield variation had been ±10%. At the end of winter, losses were up to 30–50% of the hives, compared with the usual 5–10%.[1]

Beekeepers alarmed by the amount of bees dying near industrially sown sunflowers began asking questions: they wanted more information from Bayer about the chemical's potential toxicity to the honeybee. The company presented more research but had concentrated on field and semi-field (under-tunnel) tests using prior established approaches intended for broad spray treatments rather than more covert seed coatings. Bayer's tests for residue chemical in pollen and nectar, measuring a minimum of 10 parts per billion (ppb), detected no trace of imidacloprid in systemically treated sunflowers. At the 4th International Conference on Pests in Agriculture in January 1997 and a meeting organised by the Association de Coordination Technique Agricole (Association of French Agricultural Research and Development Institutes) later that year, Bayer scientists presented these findings and additionally claimed, based on an estimate of honeybee tolerance to imidacloprid at 5,000 ppb, that the chemical couldn't be responsible for honeybee deaths. As the largest EU producer of sunflowers for unsaturated fat and bio-fuel, France and its farmers had much to lose from anything that might affect this profuse crop's profitability. Nevertheless, criticism of Bayer's results from beekeepers and their lawyers led to a call for public studies from 1997 to 1998 by the French government's food department within the Direction Générale de l'Alimentation (Ministry of Agriculture). Despite these tests proceeding at lower detection limits for trace neonicotinoid,[2*] the initial findings themselves were restricted in official reports to 10 ppb. Once the media revealed that the government and Bayer CropScience representatives had been in consultation over these detection limits, a scandal ensued and in 1999, after further protest, the French Minister of Agriculture placed an initial two-year suspension on imidacloprid use so

* Public tests between 1997–8 such as at the Centre Technique Interprofessionnel des Oléagineux Métropolitains (Technical Centre for Oilseed Crops): "had already estimated that detection limits much lower than 10 ppb – about 1.4 ppb – were necessary to find imidacloprid in nectar".

that more tests could be performed. In France, the precautionary principle had been applied rather than persisting with chemical use in the meantime.

Subsequent tests performed over several years ultimately confirmed that lower imidacloprid detection levels were necessary. In particular, scientists determined the importance of measuring the chemical's accumulative effects on honeybees. As prior research had concentrated on the acute lethal effects of imidacloprid at which 50% of honeybees die within 48 hours of exposure, more needed to be done to ascertain the chemical's chronic lethal and sublethal effects on bees after around 10 days exposure. The supposition from Bayer scientists that 5,000 ppb was the lowest concentration of imidacloprid that produced an observed effect on the honeybee was dramatically reduced to 20 ppb in 1999. While such minuscule units are already difficult to perceive, the difference between these numbers is certainly tangible; advice would be different if a person weighing 60kg (9st 6lbs) could tolerate 45mg/kg of inorganic arsenic per day as opposed to only 0.18mg/kg.[3]* Despite such a striking reassessment of the company's estimate of honeybee tolerance to neonicotinoid, Bayer could still claim that imidacloprid had no effect on honeybees if neonicotinoid remained untraceable in pollen and nectar. Tests had already proven after all that no residue imidacloprid was evident at 10 ppb, so a tolerance of 20 ppb was still officially acceptable. From 1999 to 2000, while Bayer scientists investigated the sublethal or ongoing effects of imidacloprid on honeybees by exposing them only once to the chemical and observing their response, public scientists exposed them to imidacloprid several times. While Bayer scientists were investigating the most imidacloprid a bee can consume in a single dose before its actions will be impaired, public research was replicating the foraging pattern of bees by using multiple chemical doses. Different methodology and protocols

* Based on the limit of 3.0ug/kg or 3 ppb body weight per day set by the Expert Committee on Food Additives in 2010.

returned different results: Bayer scientists measured the highest amount of imidacloprid that had no observed effect on honeybees in a range from 10-128 ppb[4] and yet public scientists found the lowest observed effect of imidacloprid from 3-12.5 ppb.[5] Evidence of neonicotinoid residues in pollen and nectar under 10 ppb was now clear. Even more importantly, public scientists had found a connection between imidacloprid residues in nectar and pollen and the honeybee's reduced ability to function as a social insect after repeatedly ingesting trace neonicotinoid.

The compound results of lower-level chemical residue and its impact on honeybee behaviour, physiology and immune system indicated that previous research had been too narrow. As honeybees consume differently depending on their caste and stage of development, studies that had previously concentrated on foragers were considered restrictive in understanding imidacloprid's effect on the health of entire colonies. While pollen foragers never consume what they collect, higher concentrations of imidacloprid in pollen would impact pollen-processing nurse bees. If nurse bee numbers reduce in the hive, fewer bees mature to become foragers, the queen is forced to lay more eggs and yet there are less bees to care for the growing larvae: as a result, the colony is imbalanced. Nectar foragers, meanwhile, that eat different amounts of honey or nectar depending on the distances they travel, would consume varying concentrations of imidacloprid. Additionally, if the colony survives the foraging season, winter bees could suffer even more damage from the chemical by ultimately ingesting quantities of imidacloprid remaining in a colony's food store. Sublethal effects of chemical poisoning therefore affect the colony as a whole: testing one bee from one colony or even several bees from several colonies can't possibly reflect the variation of possible outcomes from such dynamic social creatures. As every beekeeper knows, each colony, even within the same apiary, is distinct and differs depending on the time of year. Studies solely focused on field trials therefore ran the risk of being inconclusive, as Maxim and van der Sluijs clarify:

The principle of an experiment is to vary one factor, keeping all the others constant. This cannot be done in current field experiments with bees, because the combination of abiotic [e.g. temperature] and – especially – biotic [e.g. forage] is never identical in control fields (where the insecticide has not been used) and test fields. Bee colonies themselves are not identical, and the food sources available in the environment for honeybees are always diverse.[6]

Whereas in the 1960s Rachel Carson reflected on the lack of adequate research including field trials, Maxim and van der Sluijs consider that honeybees present too many variables for field trials to represent realistic toxicity limits. Both detection limits and test methods have had to alter significantly since the introduction of neonicotinoids. As more French researchers investigated the acute and chronic sublethal effects of imidacloprid use on colonies – initially a glaring omission from Bayer CropScience research – they found that the ongoing impact of neonicotinoid residues had been underestimated. As a result, although debate was still fierce, the French government continued to renew its suspension of imidacloprid use on sunflower seed and in 2004 extended the precautionary principle to include imidacloprid-treated corn seed as well.

By 2008, the circumstances surrounding considerable honeybee losses in Germany implied that decisions in France had been prudent. Towards the end of April, at a time when honeybees are usually starting to build their colonies, bees were dying day by day in the sunny south-west province of Baden-Württemberg. Beekeepers, who had been struggling with depleted honeybee colonies since the winter of 2003–4, suspected another chemical from the neonicotinoid class to be the cause of their problems, namely clothianidin, sold by Bayer CropScience as Poncho, a systemic seed treatment against the western corn rootworm. *Diabrotica virgifera virgifera*, which is actually a beetle that in its larval stage feeds on the roots of corn plants, was transported into Europe from the US on various sporadic occasions from the 1980s onwards.[7] Despite being a widespread pest greatly exacerbated by intensive and repetitive corn cropping in the US, the corn rootworm has so far proven a less virulent problem in Europe.[8] Just as imidacloprid had been used in advance of aphid infestation in France, however, clothianidin was also being used against corn rootworm prior to infestation, and often detection, in Europe. While corn rootworm was present at that time in Baden-Württemberg, clothianidin's impact on the honeybee would prove to be the chemical's more emphatic result. Rather than dying at pollination time, bees in this instance were notably affected at the moment when chemically treated seeds were being sown. The sudden loss of so many bees prompted Germany's Bundesamt für Verbraucherschutz und Lebensmittelsicherheit (Federal Office of Consumer Protection and Food Safety) to instruct scientists from four institutions[*] to conduct emergency tests along the Rhine valley. Consequently, a large team of public scientists at the Landwirtschaftliches Technologiezentrum (LTZ, Agricultural Technology Centre), Augustenberg, ran intensive experiments to test and analyse honeybee colonies and their sources of forage in order to discover why bees were dying so dramatically.

Armin Trenkle

Agricultural scientist, LTZ, Baden-Württemberg, Germany

From within a labyrinthine room of glass and greenery, Armin Trenkle requests five more minutes. Although the door is only

[*] Julius-Kühn Institut, Braunschweig Berlin; Landwirtschaftliche Untersuchungs- und Forschungsanstalt, Speyer; Landesanstalt für Bienenkunde, Universität Hohenheim; Landwirtschaftliches Technologiezentrum, Augustenberg.

briefly ajar, the air inside, reminiscent of botanical gardens, fills the hallway. That humidity, a familiar yet absolute otherworldliness, neatly yet incongruously housed in the middle of towns and cities, emanates from the basement of this apartment block on the outskirts of Karlsruhe. I wonder exactly what's inside, and as Annarosa Trenkle gently closes the door she reveals that her husband's almost done with the turtles and will join us upstairs shortly.

When Armin appears, he relaxes into the comfort of his living room, facing a conservatory of yet more botany, and recalls the spring of 2008. As an established LTZ member of staff since 1981, he has obviously seen many studies, and yet recalls the circumstances of honeybee colony decline specifically. To aid comprehension, Armin starts up his laptop and opens several presentations on screen. I learn more specifics about the sequence of events. Initial alerts raised by concerned beekeepers throughout the Upper Rhine region on 26th April led the German government to rapidly assign investigations of both colony losses and clothianidin use.[9] A large staff, ample facilities and LTZ's location close to the Rhine, ideally positioned the centre for a quick response to testing the area and, from a group of 100 scientific staff, Armin was duly allocated the analysis of data from tests quantifying systemic insecticide residues in bees, honey, bee bread,* pollen and flowering plants.

Together we study diagrams representative of apiaries along the Upper Rhine where scientists immediately recorded severe mortality rates. On 29th April, testing began with a series of samples collected from apiaries between Rastatt and Lörrach. At each location, handfuls of dead bees were discovered lying contorted at short distances from their hives; the dead bees, a mix of foragers and other workers that wouldn't normally leave the hive, had seemingly crawled away from their hives en-mass having abandoned their honeycomb. The brood that remained

* the food produced from pollen for larvae

in hives was extremely defective: light, deformed pupae were either found dead or severely afflicted. At the time, honeybees continued to die daily until eventually a total 12,174 colonies had been affected by similar circumstances. By the end of the onslaught, on average two-thirds of the stock from over 736 beekeepers had been devastated.[10]

Within six weeks of the first report from beekeepers, a series of tests were conducted and initial analysis submitted to the local authority. After a week prioritising bee samples, scientists then gathered pollen samples from two sources, one from an oilseed rape location, and another from apple blossom and dandelion flowers. Two days later, experts were able to discuss the results of tests evidencing the presence of clothianidin in both the initial plant sample and 98.4% of bee samples, as outlined in Armin's analysis paper.[11]* The highest level of clothianidin was measured in dandelion flowers at 113μg/kg, where 20μg/kg – equivalent to 20 ppb – was considered toxic to bees at the time.[12] Further tests discovered significant residues of clothianidin in bee bread. In total, 18 analyses (15.4%) contained more than 20 ppb of clothianidin with the highest measurement reaching 77 ppb.[13] The initial investigation therefore conclusively proved that nectar and pollen had been contaminated with clothianidin and subsequently collected, processed and transmitted within colonies to ruinous effect.

Importantly, Armin's report on honeybee losses that spring reveals a clear causal sequence of events. Although clothianidin had been used as a corn seed treatment in previous years, a significant difference occurred in the use of the systemic in 2008. The chemical, normally applied to

---

*Clothianidin was detected above NOEL (no observed effect level) in 15 plant samples (14.2%). Although the majority of bee samples contained sublethal levels of clothianidin, it was acknowledged that severely poisoned bees would have been unlikely to return to the hive.

seed with a glue-like substance known as a 'sticker', had been badly processed that year and chemical dust lay loose inside seed sacks. Of 38 sacks tested, the amount of dust varied greatly, depending to some degree even upon the level of abrasion caused by different sack material.[14] Additionally, the possibility that chemicals intended for ground distribution could become airborne had been underestimated in relation to seed sowing methods. Although tractors aren't yet a passion of mine, I'm intrigued to see the photos Armin shows me of the machines that had been routinely used to sow systemic seed. As another factor determining the dispersal of clothianidin that April concerned the effectiveness of tractor-drawn pneumatic seed drills, scientists from LTZ also ran tests on models of farm machinery. Pneumatic seed drills use an air pump mechanism to insert seed kernels into the ground and this creates exhaust as part of the process. The standard machines in use at the time returned this exhaust into the air and therefore any loose chemical had also been dispersed on the wind. Clothianidin dust had been consequently blown across nearby meadows and transmitted to flowering plants. Tests recorded the distribution of dust drift up to 30m away from the location where seed had been sown.[15] A processing error in dressing corn seed in combination with machinery exhaust had resulted in a noxious dispersal of clothianidin.

LTZ's final report corroborated what beekeepers had therefore feared all along: Poncho had emphatically been the cause of bee mortality that spring. The centre advised an outright ban on corn seed treated with clothianidin and recommended the suspension of imidacloprid and another neonicotinoid called thiamethoxam. On 15th May 2008, the German government suspended neonicotinoid licenses, placing particularly stringent restrictions on clothianidin use, and instructed public institutions such as the LTZ to continue performing tests in order to check compliance with the ruling.[16]*

After the incident in Baden-Württemberg, Bayer CropScience predictably asserted that unusual circumstances had caused chaos rather than the lethal potential of clothianidin, and yet ultimately assumed responsibility for these honeybee losses. Initially Bayer blamed the seed companies that had processed Poncho Pro and cited higher than average winds as an additional factor. At the official hearing of experts in Karlsruhe on 20th June 2008, Bayer persisted with the supposition that clothianidin is safe for bees, the environment, users and consumers "if used properly".[17] By the end of the year, however, the final report by Germany's Ministerium für Ernährung und Ländlichen Raum (Ministry for Food and Rural Areas) included clear indication that Bayer, as the manufacturer of clothianidin, was culpable for honeybee poisoning. During 2008, in consultation with the Regional Ministry, Freiburg Regional Authority and Baden-Württemberg District Administration, Bayer CropScience organised a swift, out-of-court settlement of €2.25million to local beekeepers.[18]

Although this financial payment necessarily acknowledged the gravity of sudden honeybee losses, the future of German beekeeping would also be influenced by the government's long-term agrochemical strategy. In the same report, as conclusion, the Regional Ministry outlined its recommendations for seed dressings that called for stricter technical specifications, guidelines for proper use and monitoring programmes. Although clothianidin had already been suspended, the emphasis in this report was therefore on means to regulate chemical use rather than to reduce overall environmental toxicity. Notably, based on

---

* Subsequent checks in 2009 proved that only one in ten farmers had contravened the ruling, as indicated by significantly lower-levels of neonicotinoids in plant samples: only 0.02% clothianidin, 0.04% imidacloprid and 0.025% thiamethoxam were recorded in the first year post-suspension.

the investigations of LTZ and other institutions, the Ministry advised the conversion of seed drills to reduce dust drift. Alongside pictures of standard seed drills, labelled 'Machinery Type A', Armin's laptop displays images of 'Machinery Type B and C': the former being a conversion of 'A' and the latter a new model tractor, both intended to return exhaust and any dust drift into the ground. As Armin and I look at further slides illustrating the performance of seed drills, I'm disconcerted by the harsh realities indicated by one graph in particular. Three coloured lines chart the dispersal of dust drift from the different sowing machines and points of interconnected luminous purple, depicting adapted 'Machine B', scale the diagram in front of me almost as violently as those indicating the machine before its extra cap has been fitted. The cheap, quick fix doesn't look at all convincing. A striking yellow line that flashes to the fore, meanwhile, measures the total insertion of chemicals below ground by new, improved 'Machine C' and this doesn't look reassuring either.[19] Out of sight surely shouldn't mean out of mind where chemicals are concerned; while neonicotinoid poisoning had proven tangible to an insect that we're overtly aware of, these chemicals are of course intentionally toxic to small life forms and likely affect other beneficial insects. As Armin and I finish looking through his data from 2008, it occurs to me that this was a truly shocking incident not only in relation to the honeybee but also as indication of broader environmental damage. Asking questions is accumulative, as are neonicotinoids in soil, and I now had more questions rather than less about the sense of governing for short-term profit over long-term prosperity, business over environment, corn farmer over beekeeper.

Although the suspension of neonicotinoids in Germany was rapidly and purposefully enforced, the ruling was accompanied by several governmental concessions enabling farming to continue relatively unrestricted. The risk of loose chemical dust wasn't considered as much of a threat to other systemic seed production and some decisions were near instantaneously made to re-establish clothianidin use, specifically as a dressing for oilseed rape;[20] although honeybees feed from rapeseed plants, it was considered that without dust drift the neonicotinoid would be safe as a systemic treatment in this instance. As one of the largest producers of corn in the EU, replacement options were also considered necessary so that intensive production could continue: a chemical substitute for clothianidin was reauthorised for use throughout Germany.[21]* Alterations to seed drill machinery subsequently changed national procedure, which then influenced an EU-wide mandate in 2010 to reduce and ultimately eliminate any dust drift produced by seed drill machinery. While certain lines had been drawn regarding neonicotinoid use, grey areas concerning where, how and on what they could be used persisted.

Meanwhile, despite restrictions in Bayer's home country, clothianidin was still an officially authorised product; Bayer CropScience, one of the largest agrochemical companies worldwide, was still free to trade Poncho and other neonicotinoid products elsewhere in the EU. Marketing material for Poncho maintained that clothinaidin's benefits were "in the bag": as a systemic seed treatment, Bayer focused on the assertion that "the farmer is considerably less exposed to this product" especially in comparison with "chemical classes of organophosphates, pyrethroids and fiproles, which are known to be more toxic than Poncho".[22] Indeed, one of the main marketing strategies for clothianidin appears to have been that it's not as toxic as chemicals already largely sidelined. Comparatives such as 'more' or 'less' in no way refute the existence of toxicity and exposure,

*The carbonate, methiocarb, which in May 2008 had been banned in Germany, was reinstated for use with corn on 9th Feb 2009.

however, and reduced risk had already proven to be a selective principle where clothianidin was concerned. Poncho, suggestive in name of a protective blanket for both farmer and crop, was revealing itself to be more of a poisonous drape. Despite decades of standard regulatory protocol regarding general chemical use in the EU, few restrictions had been developed to specifically protect pollinator health. Although after events in Baden-Württemberg the extent of clothianidin's potential toxicity to honeybees was literally and metaphorically 'out of the bag', at this point no EU-wide precautionary principle was applied to neonicotinoid use.

Around the time of Germany's neonicotinoid suspension, other EU countries did independently ban clothianidin, however. In 2008, a few months prior to contamination in Germany, France refused Bayer's registration proposal for clothianidin as a corn seed treatment; Italy banned the chemical's use on corn that same year; Slovenia, meanwhile, banned the use of clothianidin on corn due to bee poisonings in 2008 and again in 2011 after the chemical's license had been reinstated and yet subsequently led to a further incident of bee losses. Although France and Italy, like Germany, are renowned for significant corn production, these governments were willing to suspend neonicotinoid use despite negative assertions – generally from agrochemical companies – that yield and profit would suffer.

Not all European governments changed their position on crop protection in favour of pollinator protection, however. Just across the border from Germany in Austria, for example, scientists studying ongoing incidences of honeybee deaths at the Agentur für Gesundheit und Ernährungssicherheit (AGES, Agency for Health and Food Security) were required to find their own proof of neonicotinoid toxicity. Bayer's suggestion that the incident at Baden-Württemberg had been an isolated incident was treated with suspicion, but nevertheless the possibility that honeybee decline, still popularly known as Colony Collapse Disorder, might be caused by other factors such as parasites and viruses required thorough investigation.

Hemma Köglberger
Small-scale beekeeper and agricultural scientist, AGES
Lower Austria, Austria

I've arranged to meet Hemma Köglberger, leading AGES researcher of honeybee viruses, at her home near Vienna. Today happens to be by far the hottest this year and, in this open agricultural landscape, there's precious little shade. As I pass through the garden gate, two young boys are just visible between the intense blue of a high-sided paddling pool and the wide, cloudless sky above. Hemma, who at that moment appears from the house, motions me towards the cover of some trailing vines where I'm soon sipping homemade cordial and eating loganberries from the garden. With relaxed enthusiasm, she suggests we could visit her hives and so, despite the heat, I find myself keenly setting off back through the gate and down the road past broad fields of ripening cereal crops.

Although I can't see it through the towering corn, we're walking in the vicinity of Europe's largest river. The Danube had shown its might in two recent floods, the first of which resulted in one local beekeeper losing all of their hives to rising water in 2002. As hives in these flatlands need protection from stormy weather, Hemma – the first of three beekeepers in the immediate area – locates her hives in a discreet position behind a wood stack under a few isolated trees. As is often the case with beekeeping, Hemma's bees occupy someone else's land.

As we approach the hives, I'm warned that the insects most keenly interested in our arrival will be mosquitoes rather then bees. Hemma, who collects honey in the company of these parasitic insects every year, is coolly coping with the summer onslaught, but we're decidedly outnumbered and soon the voracious mosquitoes get the better of us. On this occasion, for my benefit, she decides to let them win and we make our way back to the house without having seen the bees. On our return, as if in consolation, we're greeted by Hemma's son and his friend who've also been out exploring. They're clutching a few ears of corn collected from neighbouring fields: easy pickings, like we'd been for the mosquitoes.

* * *

Later that day, the first topic Hemma and I speak of in relation to her honeybee research at AGES is the use of clothianidin as a treatment against corn rootworm. As in Germany, scientists in Austria have been intensely involved in research related to the insecticide since 2008, but unlike their colleagues across the border they've been somewhat restricted by the equipment in their lab. At AGES, although researchers receive plenty of dead bee samples from worried beekeepers with cornfields near their hives, the institute is unable to directly investigate the situation. As the pesticide is highly potent and can be manufactured at an incredibly low-level concentration, it is complex work detecting residues that may remain on the bees or in their hives. "A method is being developed, which makes the research very expensive. [Meanwhile] it is very difficult to find a lab [to test samples], because there are not so many that can do it. ... In Germany there were approved cases of bee losses in connection with the sowing of maize seed, [but] they have problems again this year and have to work on their own samples." I ask if each country has to prove the detrimental effect of any agricultural chemical: "In Austria there are some restrictions on use now, but they think it [the insecticide] can be managed by changing the method of sowing the prepared seed." It would appear that legislators within each EU country may not need their own proof but can pick and choose how to interpret evidence uncovered elsewhere.

Hemma's main research involves the search for means to investigate viruses, which are equally difficult to detect and can also be deadly to the honeybee. There are currently eighteen viruses known to affect *Apis mellifera*, of which only seven can be tested. 'Deformed Wing Virus', 'Acute Bee Paralysis Virus', 'Black Queen Cell Virus' and 'Chronic Bee Paralysis Virus' have all been identified in relation to honeybees, for example, using Polymerase Chain Reaction methods that multiply genetic information. Not all of the viruses known to affect honeybees may be harmful – just as some viruses may be benign to humans – but identifying the range of honeybee viral infections is vital to our understanding of what shapes bee health.

Further knowledge of parasites is also important. Of particular interest right now is the newly identified fungal parasite, *Nosema ceranae*, which was discovered on *Apis mellifera* in 2007 and the year before on *Apis ceranae*, the small forest honeybee from Asia. In recent years, tests on samples predating the discovery of *Nosema ceranae* have resulted in evidence of the parasite existing in honeybees in Austria since 2003. At a recent conference, Hemma also heard of samples in Poland that evidence nosema infestations in honeybees from as early as 1995. The parasite, which shares attributes with the earlier known honeybee disease, *Nosema apis*, affects the intestines of bees. However, unlike *Nosema apis* – which has seemingly all but disappeared since the year 2000 – *Nosema ceranae* can live on in colonies all year round, making it a highly-prolific parasite. One noted effect of infected colonies is the total disappearance of bees from their hives, leaving them empty but full of honey. With stories of recent colony losses still in mind, it's hard not to draw immediate conclusions: Could *Nosema ceranae* and Colony Collapse Disorder be one and the same thing?

As Hemma continues to discuss the issues affecting bee health, however, it soon becomes apparent that more than one known parasite can produce this behaviour. In fact, Hemma and her colleagues don't officially recognise the term Colony Collapse Disorder and prefer to term what they investigate as 'unclarified bee losses'. For example, vulnerable bees heavily infested by *Varroa destructor* that consequently succumb to Acute Bee Paralysis Virus have also been known to disappear from their hives. Varroa, the parasite perhaps best known to all beekeepers, can initially be difficult to detect in the hive, as the mite infects colonies by laying eggs within brood cells that contain bee larvae, especially male drone cells that gestate for longer. In each cell, an occupying female varroa mite lays six eggs: the first, containing a male, hatches and mates with all subsequent females as they hatch. When the young bee finally emerges from its cell, it carries the fertile mites throughout the colony, which can then move from one bee to another, sucking haemolymph for food before entering other brood cells to multiply further. As the relatively large, orange-domed varroa carapaces grow alongside the hive's increasing brood through spring and summer into autumn, the parasite becomes more and more virulent from late summer onwards and often proves deadly to honeybee colonies over winter. Like *Nosema ceranae*, it too is a significant adversary.

Instead of the European honeybee slowly adapting to varroa, the mite's impact has in fact become all the more critical over time. As Hemma says, in Austria, where varroa was first noted in 1986, records of 10,000 mites per colony were common and yet such high-level infestation did not necessarily result in the total destruction of a colony. By 2004, however, lower-level infestations of 3,000 mites were enough to heavily endanger an entire hive. In the interim period, it would appear that something had lowered the bee's tolerance. Researchers at the time considered the heightened risk to bee health could be due to increased attack from viruses, which can be transported from one honeybee to another via the mite, but could something else have also reduced the bee's immune system?

Rather than having no clues as to why honeybees are disappearing and dying in vast numbers, it would seem there are actually many factors that can affect similar outcomes. The precise cause of honeybee deaths is elusive not because of an unknown culprit but due to the amount of variants at play. Although scientists may not have categorically identified all viruses and parasites, multi-factorial diseases and a range of external influences are already evidently affecting the honeybee. The trick is to be able to discern which combination is causal. Varroa, when mature, may be easy to spot without a microscope, but Acute Bee Paralysis Virus is not. Bee corpses may sometimes be locatable, but potential residue chemicals in their system are increasingly complicated to identify due to the way they are manufactured.

"The main thing has become proof", intones Hemma. Although many aspects determine bee health, it's telling that she pinpoints the product that lies covertly within the corncobs gleaned from the field by her son: "I think in some cases it is hard to believe there is no connection between the use of chemicals in agriculture and colony damage. Nevertheless, it's difficult if you can't prove it." Despite remaining diplomatic and measured as we speak about subjects clearly critical to Hemma's research, at this point she underlines her position by asserting "… we would like to prove it."

⁓

From 2009 to 2011, research undertaken by agricultural scientists at AGES was aimed at doing just that: in response to ongoing reports of weakening honeybee colonies in Austria, the MELISSA project published in 2012 developed "investigations in the incidence of bee losses in corn and oilseed rape growing areas of Austria and possible correlations with bee diseases and the use of insecticidal plant protection products". Symptoms of honeybee losses that had prompted the study evidenced:

> ... increased bee mortality, symptoms of acute
> intoxication, flightless bees, crawlers, clustered
> groups of flightless bees in the grass in front of the
> hives, trembling bees, decrease in colony strength and
> in a few cases the removal of dead bee brood.[23]

In order to evaluate the causes of such extreme effects, scientists sampled dead bees, bee bread, honey, systemic seeds and plants for residue chemical traces from areas where beekeepers had reported bee losses. They also tested bee samples for parasites and pathogens. Analysis of residue insecticide returned evidence of trace neonicotinoids in significant measure. As in Baden-Württemberg, Germany, all samples other than honey tested positive for neonicotinoid.[24]*

Significant neonicotinoid contamination evident throughout the research period was associated with dust drift. Analysis from 2009, indicative of all three years' research, details that:

> The appearance of honeybees showing symptoms of
> poisoning coincided to a high degree with the corn
> sowing period, which overlapped with the spring bloom
> period of fruit trees, dandelion, hedges and meadow.[25]

---

* As bees act as a 'filter' by processing nectar, there may have been no contaminant found in honey but AGES recorded that 83% of bee samples, 65% of bee bread and all plant samples tested positive for neonicotinoid residues in the first year. By 2010, AGES recorded 51% clothianidin, 23% thiamethoxam, 14% fipronil, 9% fipronil sulfone and no imidacloprid in 89 samples. Concentrations of insecticide in bee bread tested the same year also implicated clothianidin as the worst offender: 34 samples taken after corn had been sown tested 74% positive for the neonicotinoid. Overall in 2010, bee bread tested from apiaries where poisoning was suspected returned twice as much contaminant – either clothianidin or thiamethoxam – than from control sites. Although summary analysis suggests that the overall levels of neonicotinoid residues found in bee and bee bread samples had reduced from 2009–2011, it was also noted that incidences of imidacloprid use had developed exponentially in just one year.

The AGES questionnaire "surveying sowing conditions and type of maize and oilseed pumpkin seed used" also returned results suggestive of varied engagement with bee-friendly farming techniques. In evaluation, AGES considered that frequently missing answers to particular questions "suggested the need for further information and improvements, e.g. concerning the use of sowing machines with deflectors, the need to observe the binding provisions regarding sowing under windy conditions or to avoid drift contamination of flowering off crop areas."[26] Although the EU's regulatory amendment for clothianidin use in 2010 had reduced dust drift, its aim to eliminate contamination by monitoring machinery alone hadn't been successful.

Whereas it's generally considered that legislation is necessary to change mainstream behaviour, the most encouraging detail from the MELISSA report therefore relates to the independent action of arable farmers in Austria during the final year of study. Despite the suspension of neonicotinoids in three neighbouring countries, Austria retained its chemical licenses and yet:

> In 2011, sales of seeds with insecticidal dressing decreased in Austria by about one third, compared to 2010, whereas the maize growing area considerably increased to approximately 297,000 ha.[27]

A significant number of agricultural businesses had chosen ahead of legislation to discontinue treatments that were proving increasingly unreliable and unpopular. The overall reduction in neonicotinoid residues found by AGES by 2011 must therefore in part be due to this notable step away from specific chemical use. After all, one reasonable means of minimising chemical use is to reduce demand.

In addition to the evidence of dust drift, analysis of bee samples from affected sites importantly concluded that none of the cases monitored could have been directly caused by parasitic or viral infections. From 2009 onwards, it was noted that:

> The examination of samples of dead bees derived
> from bee yards [apiaries] with suspected poisoning
> gave positive evidence only for some of the pathogens
> and parasites investigated and for some of the affected
> bee yards, indicating that the observed symptoms
> were not linked to bee pathogens or parasites.[28]

Such findings at AGES supported those already established by scientists at the Julius-Kühn Institut, Germany, who'd also investigated honeybee decline in Baden-Württemberg and categorically stated in relation to neonicotinoid use and high-level bee mortality that: "No correlation with any bee pathogens was detected."[29] Where systemically treated corn and other monoculture crops are grown, it's important to underline that neonicotinoid use has variously been the primary cause of bee losses. In addition, other studies, such as those published in Environmental Biology, 2009, and PLoS ONE, 2013, have identified instances where the presence of neonicotinoid exacerbates existing disease, suggesting that these chemicals are indeed catalysts of bee disease in more ways than one.[30*]

Although the MELISSA project in its entirety formed significant argument for the suspension of neonicotinoid use in Austria, when submitted to government it had little immediate impact. Despite being publicly funded, the research had been produced at an institution that also represents agricultural practices under scrutiny within the report and this conflict of interest may well have made action more complicated. As no legislative change was forthcoming at national level, beekeepers and scientists had to hope that the report would have more effect at the European Commission.

In 2012, the EC asked the European Food Safety Authority

---

* Scientific evidence links nosema infection to increased neonicotinoid ingestion rates where chemicals are present, which in turn significantly reduces the honeybee's immunity to pathogens.

(EFSA) to compile a review that would analyse the impact of neonicotinoid use on honeybees in order to clarify the validity of their authorisation as agricultural chemicals. The MELISSA project and other studies from various EU countries would be assessed alongside research that had in part sparked the review. Of all the peer-reviewed studies compiled about systemic chemicals, two papers in particular – both published in the internationally-renowned journal *Science* that year – had encouraged the EC to act: one produced by the University of Stirling and Lancaster University correlates significant bumblebee colony impairment and queen losses with imidacloprid; the other, a French study, details the homing failure of honeybees exposed to non-lethal doses of thiamethoxam.[31] With these two studies, the debate surrounding neonicotinoid use had expanded to encompass more than the immediate and acute mortality of honeybees. After only six years of registration, clothianidin (Bayer CropScience) was attracting close scrutiny – alongside imidacloprid (Bayer CropScience), thiamethoxam (Syngenta) and other chemicals within the neonicotinoid class – which the EC considered required collating and cross-referencing.

The studies the authority assessed, although not all conclusive, were indication that broad investigation of the long-term effects neonicotinoids have on pollinators was necessary. The EFSA's Pesticide Peer Review states:

> Several issues that could not be finalised were identified in relation to the exposure of honey bees via dust, from consumption of contaminated nectar and pollen, and from residues in exposure via guttation fluid [sap from plant leaves]. In addition, the risk to pollinators other than honey bees, the risk from insect honeydew [aphid secretions], and the risk from exposure to residues in succeeding crops could not be finalised.[32]

As a set of potentially toxic factors, the EFSA's points of concern form a critical list of ways bees could be poisoned that reads not unlike the "weird world" described by Rachel Carson over fifty years ago. If all aspects mentioned ultimately prove noxious, the honeybee would be under strain from all sources of nutrition, whether ingesting nectar and pollen from systemically treated plants or those tainted with chemical dust, taking up toxins from the sap exuded from systemically treated plants, or from the plants ingested and secreted by aphids. If next year's plants also take up chemical residues remaining in soil, they may augment yet another tainted dose when least expected. Ultimately, these accumulative circumstances would leave the honeybee and other pollinators little respite, especially given the following 'critical areas of concern':

> A high acute risk to honeybees was identified from exposure via dust drift for the seed treatment uses in maize, oilseed rape and cereals. A high acute risk was also identified from exposure via residues in nectar and / or pollen for the uses in oilseed rape.[33]

Despite challenges from Bayer and Syngenta regarding the content of the EFSA's conclusions, the EC stood firmly by its review and evidence that neonicotinoid dust drift and residues in nectar and pollen are high acute risks to honeybees. In January 2013, the commission proposed a two-year suspension of imidacloprid, clothianidin and thiamethoxam so that thorough neonicotinoid research could be undertaken. This new class of pesticides, as with synthetic chemicals of the past, seemed to be following a remarkably familiar sequence of events. Two months later, the proposal was presented to representatives of all EU member states and went to a vote. Although 13 countries were in favour of the ban, 9 were against, while 5 countries, including Germany and the UK, abstained from voting.* Without a firm majority in either direction, the EC began preparations for a second round vote.

In response, both Syngenta and Bayer CropScience sent various letters to the commission presenting their cases for the continuation of neonicotinoid authorisation. Of the six main players within the global biotechnology market, Syngenta – the sole producer of thiamethoxam – and Bayer CropScience – which patented the first commercial neonicotinoid, imidacloprid, and owns key rights to the production of clothianidin – are of particular note here as both companies profit significantly from their neonicotinoid research, production and distribution.[34]† The letter that Syngenta sent to Commissioner John Dalli canvassed for support in particular regarding the French Minister of Agriculture's intention to ban Cruiser OSR, a thiamethoxam systemic for oilseed rape. The letter emphasises the company's meeting with G8 members and Syngenta's commitment to spend millions of dollars towards global food security, especially in Africa, as if a charitable carrot bartered

*In the first round ministerial vote, the 13 EU countries in favour were France, Italy, Slovenia, Spain, Sweden, Poland, the Netherlands, Luxembourg, Denmark, Cyprus, Belgium, Latvia and Malta; the 9 against were Ireland, Hungary, Czech Republic, Slovakia, Romania, Portugal, Austria, Lithuania and Greece; the 5 that abstained were the UK, Germany, Bulgaria, Estonia and Finland.

† From the ten largest companies that controlled 80–90% of the global agricultural chemical market in 1997–8, half formed the conglomerations of Bayer Crop Science and Syngenta. In the very same year that France banned the Bayer product, Gaucho, as a sunflower seed treatment, AgrEvo, a conglomerate of two German crop protection companies, merged with French pharmaceutical and chemical company, Rhône-Poulenc, to form Aventis CropScience. Just three years later, Aventis 'CropScience' was acquired by Bayer AG, which merged its Crop Protection division into Bayer CropScience. Also in 1999, Swedish company Astra AB merged with UK company Zeneca Group to become Astra-Zeneca. In 2000, Novartis, based in Basel, Switzerland, and Astra-Zeneca merged to form Syngenta. Along with Monsanto (USA), BASF (Germany), Dow-Agrosciences LLC (USA) and DuPont Pioneer (USA), Syngenta and Bayer CropScience form the six-founder company membership of the Council for Biotechnological Information.

against neonicotinoid authorisation. The writer references the fact that "G8 members were urged to support progressive principles, including robust regulatory frameworks, to best enable food security... [by] ...Research and Development companies like ours", as if Syngenta might withdraw funding should the precautionary principle be applied. Page two of the letter states: "I recognise that some Member States, driven by a small group of activists and hobby beekeepers, are lobbying you to suspend Cruiser OSR and indeed the entire class of neonicotinoids",[35] which in no way disguises an obvious attempt to discredit the beekeeping farming sector and its representatives. Referring to beekeepers as hobbyists, regardless of whether they are indeed professional, is a blunt stab at experienced beekeepers burdened by increasing difficulties within their practices.

A more positive attitude to beekeepers and their role in farming policy recognises the central role professional practitioners have in providing valuable practical knowledge and information in support of thorough research. Maxim and van der Sluijs, when concluding their 2012 findings based on French practitioners in relation to an earlier report from the European Environment Agency, state:

> Another important lesson from the first volume of *Late lessons from early warnings* is the need to 'Ensure the use of "lay" and local knowledge, as well as relevant specialist expertise in the appraisal' (EEA, 2001) ... the experience of honeybee colony decline in France shows that bodies performing monitoring studies should have the trust and the acceptance of the field actors directly concerned (in our case, beekeepers and farmers). From the first alert, particular attention should have been given to the professional beekeepers, who have daily experience and good knowledge of the land and of the insects they breed.[36]

While Syngenta's arrogant posturing dared to belittle beekeepers, Bayer CropScience noticeably took a different stance in relation to the suspension. Having already compensated beekeepers for losses incurred through chemical mismanagement in Baden-Württemberg, it would have been difficult for Bayer CropScience to target them in any way regarding their concerns over chemical use. When a Bayer representative wrote a letter to Commissioner Dalli just four days after Syngenta, their rhetoric was inclined towards the accusation of others instead:

> During the past years there have been a number of incidents which have had an effect on honeybees – but almost all of them were a result of inappropriate use and / or lack of application precaution.[37]

Although non-explicit, Bayer's sentiment implicates farmers and seed production companies for the mismanagement of their products. Any responsibility for significant honeybee mortality caused by clothianidin dust drift is juxtaposed later in the same letter by Bayer's suggestion that:

> … for our company the safety of bees is a top priority. Since the unfortunate accident in the south-west of Germany a few years ago we are heavily investing into research, machinery and stewardship measures … We are committed, together with member states and the Commission, to develop and implement all necessary measures to prevent any avoidable negative impact on the environment and have the best available solutions for the European farmers.[38]

Of course, Bayer doesn't acknowledge that "European farmers" could legitimately include beekeepers and that one of "the best available solutions" for European bee farmers might be the withdrawal of neonicotinoids. However, the seed production companies anonymously implicated in Bayer's statement, highlight the difficulty of pinpointing responsibility when so many subsidiaries are involved in a corporate agricultural chain. As chemical companies are unlikely to pull profitable products themselves, and farmers and consumers face ongoing financial pressures, it seems increasingly necessary for lawmakers and government ministers to prioritise public and environmental health over corporate concerns.

Worryingly though, during the consultation period of the EC's proposal between EU Member States, the UK Environment Secretary sent a letter to Syngenta that highlights at least one government's diametrically opposed priorities. In response to correspondence from Syngenta on 12th April 2013, Owen Patterson wrote:

> Since the Commission indicated its intention to restrict neonicotinoids, the UK has been very active in calling for a better approach. I have raised the issue twice in the Agricultural Council and officials have also been working to explain the science and the consequences of taking the wrong action. We have argued that the Commission should withdraw their proposal and should finish the scientific assessment they have begun. We have backed up this call with our new study and assessment of the evidence sent to the Commission and to all Member States.[39]

Although the UK officially abstained from voting either for or against the proposed suspension, Patterson's comments suggest that the government was in fact "active" in campaigning against the proposal. In no uncertain terms, "the wrong action" here refers to neonicotinoid suspension and reflects the UK government's sympathies with companies such as Syngenta. Patterson's support for the biotech company is based on a disingenuous argument, however: in reality the commission was never going to "withdraw their proposal" to "finish the scientific assessment", as neither the commission nor the EFSA had further research within their remit. The aim of the Pesticide Peer Review was to collate existing studies and identify whether enough evidence of neonicotinoid-induced honeybee mortality indicated the need to suspend chemical use *in order* to perform more research. The "new study" performed by publicly-funded UK researchers was damning enough and clearly demonstrated that neonicotinoids had become so prevalent in EU farming that field trials simply couldn't be performed without a suspension: the bumblebee field experiments mentioned by Patterson were deemed worthless by the EC, as all control sites that should have been free of chemicals were contaminated with neonicotinoids.

Meanwhile, in a bid to offset the stark evidence that had been revealed by the EFSA's investigations, Bayer CropScience and Syngenta collectively launched 'Operation Pollinator'. While promoting means to continue selling neonicotinoids, the Operation Pollinator action plan otherwise centres on increasing the amount of flowering field margins alongside intensive farming. Monoculture significantly reduces rural plant diversity and the recreation of field margins should therefore increase the amount of wild flowers as well as crops that insects can feed on. Pollinators certainly require a range of forage and yet this concession is perhaps less generous than it at first appears. As strips alongside fields sown with systemic seeds might be contaminated by dust drift, Operation Pollinator flowering field margins could become high acute risk sites for those pollinators otherwise being encouraged to thrive. Within the first-tier risk assessment of the EFSA's Pesticide Peer Review, studies of "a narrow strip downwind at the edge of the treated field" equivalent to flowering field margins evidenced:

> ... that forager honeybees or other pollinators occurring in this strip are at high risk (e.g. via direct contact to dust) and may be able to carry considerable residues back to the hive (for social bees).[40]

Publicity material for Bayer's additional pro-pollinator programme, 'Bee Care' – which is a vehicle for the company's chemical products against honeybee parasites – looks especially circumspect when viewed with awareness of neonicotinoid contamination: soft-focus sunflowers interspersed with complimentary purple flowers and the odd dot of red and white no longer appear so romantic. Images of meadows and areas of mixed planting within this context can no longer be disassociated from neonicotinoid dust drift even when, as here, there's no corn in sight.

Despite concerted agrochemical company lobbying, a mass of public support for the EC's proposal of a two-year neonicotinoid suspension ultimately proved more influential. When an appeal was presented on 29th April 2013, several votes swung in favour of the proposal. Germany in particular amended its original abstention inline with public opinion, which meant that, with 15 countries in agreement of the proposal, the EC was able to apply the neonicotinoid suspension. Unlike Germany, the UK notably revised its decision and voted against the suspension, despite the failure of its bumblebee research. In Austria, meanwhile, the government's repeat vote against the suspension sparked heightened controversy for the Environment Minister: a wave of comment questioning the minister's decision and lack of transparency led to calls for his resignation. When a government document from the Food Security Department prescribing official secrecy in relation to the type and amount of agricultural chemicals used in Austria was made public, it fuelled a sustained series of headline news stories across the entire media spectrum. Alongside outrage at failed governmental protocols, a distinctive shift occurred at this time in the representation of pesticides. Tabloid front pages reinforced the broadsheet depiction of a grey figure in a nuclear age, protective suit liberally spraying a field of crops next to a colourful stack of beehives: 'plant protection products' were repeatedly heralded as "bee poison".[41] A deluge of articles asserted that the industrial agricultural lobby was an overt influence on the government and had compromised the ministerial interpretation of public research regarding pesticide toxicity and bees:

> Neonicotinoids used in agriculture as plant protection products burden the entire ecosystem and, in strong expert opinion, largely contribute to bee deaths. For Berlakovich [the Austrian Environment Minister] this hasn't been proven yet. He wants to continue sitting on the fence. In Brussels, he votes against a neonicotinoid ban on 'pure technical grounds'. He argues for the protection of farming practice over the protection of bees. Protection of the chemical, biofuel and animal feed industries interests, which need corn galore, arguably also plays a significant role.[42]

Due to the scope of environmental concern in Austria, the government's decision was considered imbalanced and Berlakovich rapidly organised a conference of experts to discuss bee health. A review of the environment and agriculture departmental structure within parliament was proposed, so that an influential agricultural perspective would be less likely to overwhelm environmental concerns in future.

Unfortunately, while dividing agricultural and environmental decision-making might appear to defend the environment from corporate lobbying, such a separation also highlights our unhealthy tendency to disassociate farming from nature. Splitting agriculture and environment issues relegates beekeeping to the periphery of both. Despite a relatively strong sense of beekeeping as farming within Austria, it's evident that the honeybee's dual characteristics as both a wild and farmed creature have allowed it to fall between categories in policymaking here as well. At a rally in support of the neonicotinoid ban outside parliament in Vienna,[43] when commercial beekeeper Stefan Mandl stated his dissatisfaction at the government's decision to support large-scale corn production over his farming practice, his words resonated loud and clear with fellow campaigners, many of whom were professional beekeepers. With 7,000 hives on the outskirts of Vienna, Mandl's beekeeping operation should be difficult to ignore, and yet he feels his practice has already been minoritised within agricultural policymaking. Although pollination is integral to the success of horticulture and beekeeping itself representative of both husbandry and harvest, apiculture tends to remain low in agriculture's hierarchy. Politics that place bee health within an environmental framework to compensate for unpopular decisions sideline the fact that bees are also relevant to agricultural business.

From 1st December 2013, clothianidin, imidacloprid and thiamethoxam were suspended as seed treatment, granular soil application and foliar treatment on plants and cereals attractive to bees for a period of two years. Based on the EFSA review, the suspension includes: "alfalfa (minor use), clover (minor use), maize (corn), mustard, oilseed rape, sunflower, poppy".[44] For a short period of time, scientists throughout the EU should at least be able to find conditions in which to ascertain the effects of a chemical class on pollinators without its overt, general use contaminating experiments. Although two years is seen as a positive start, several caveats have already been raised to balance the expectations of the suspension: neonicotinoids are known to remain in soil beyond their use and can be readily transmitted to otherwise untreated plants; they also breakdown and leach into ground water, which further disseminates the pesticides.[45] Furthermore, only crops that honeybees actively pollinate are included in the suspension. Not all plants or practices are covered and so there's rational concern that bee health may still be compromised by unanticipated events.[46]* The hope, however, is that an initial period of significantly reduced neonicotinoid use might lead to other positive readjustments of farming practices.

---

* Additionally, there are other classes of pesticide that are newly suspected to have a negative impact on bee health. Recent research, for example, has revealed that widely used fungicides, such as chlorothalonil and pyraclostrobin, can contribute significantly to honeybee intolerance to parasites.

adaptation

three

A low, reverberant hum resonates across the day's clear, even sky. As I watch the empty expanse above me, a lone cloud appears beyond the rooftops and, with a thrill, I recognise the sound and then the form of a honeybee swarm. This is the first I've ever seen in person and I'm transfixed by its movement. The bees lightly shape a ripple on the breeze, a parallel to the sway of wheat fields. Although too distant to see individually, they appear to cut the landscape as carbon copies of one another, absorbing all colour in their wake: the natural and phenomenal entwined. Hovering without apparent direction, the collection senses its way. From my perspective, this fragment of a colony, which passes as soon as it has appeared, is now heading away from the village towards the forest.

The swarm leaves me spellbound and yet, almost instantaneously, I picture the hive that must be reduced by several thousand bees. As an excitable witness, I make a quick call to the local beekeeper only to hear that he saw the swarm leave one of his four hives some ten minutes earlier. I describe the bearing the swarm has since taken and this confirms the beekeeper's loss: the bees are travelling too far into the mountains to be retrievable. This splinter group will have to fend for itself in a different location, having instinctively taken a new direction, a fresh proliferation that's also a return to the wild.

⌒

A swarm of honeybees is an intense spectacle. Although now a rare sight, even in the imagination a mass of honeybees makes a powerful impression. Despite often being a calm entity placated with honey and unified by the queen bee's pheromones, the flight of so many bees at once exacerbates our fear of being stung. We're no longer used to seeing bees nesting wild and have lost our positive association with the observation of places where honeybees might naturally choose to make their comb. Hives have long sanitised our perception of honeybees and honey production. The caretaking and maintenance beekeepers perform regulates insect behaviour so succinctly that we perceive a honeybee swarm as extraordinary. Once a colony is no longer contained within its hive, the species commonly categorised as *domitae naturae* no longer behaves as *animus revertendi* – with an intention to return – and becomes *ferea naturae*. The domesticated honeybee suddenly appears feral and beyond our control. This blurring of distinction, when considered in legal terms, also affects the ownership of honeybees, as stated by Frimston and Smith in *Beekeeping and the Law* (1993):

> Nobody would have much hesitation in saying that a beekeeper owns his hives together with the bees inside … It's a different matter when bees swarm. Swarming bees do not intend to return to the hive. The question therefore arises as to who owns a swarm of bees in the air or on the branch in a neighbour's garden.[1]

As it can be difficult to ascertain where a swarm has come from, both the rights and responsibility of the original beekeeper can suddenly become contentious.

While most beekeepers are therefore keen to avoid colonies swarming, and manage their hives accordingly, honeybees swarm as part of their natural lifecycle. Swarming regulates colony size and, even more importantly, ensures proliferation. The honeybee's breeding cycle, based on an intricate combination of circumstances and actions, results in a colony separating into two or more groups. As a coherent colony depends on the strength of the queen bee's pheromone to communicate her presence, swarm preparations commonly occur when a colony increases in size and the queen's influence therefore decreases.* The first sign of bees preparing to swarm is the production of virgin queen cups, which the queen's pheromone ordinarily suppresses. These bulbous cases protruding above the honeycomb are laid with eggs which, once hatched into larvae, are fed royal jelly by nurse bees in order to develop otherwise standard worker bees into virgin queens.† The sight of many foragers remaining in the hive is yet another indication of a colony preparing to swarm: worker bees gorge themselves on honey prior to departure so that they'll have the energy required to build new comb once relocated. The colony's mature queen is simultaneously starved of food so that she stops laying eggs and reduces her size in order to be able to fly out with the swarm. Then, about a week after this primary swarm has left the hive, virgin queens hatch from their cells and either destroy the remaining queen cups or else fight one another until only one remains. Alternatively, if the colony is still sizeable, workers may guard the remaining queen cups from already hatched virgins so that secondary swarms may also leave the hive led by these extra queens. What remains of the original colony stays where it is with a single virgin queen, which only briefly leaves the hive to mate before returning to renew colony numbers and restore the hive's productive order.

As a primary swarm initially tends to go no further than 10 metres from its hive, to a tree or other spot where only a ladder may be necessary to reach it, this is the optimum moment for a swarm to be collected and returned to the controlled *domitae* world of the hive and its beekeeper.‡ Recovery has to be performed quickly, however:

* A queen's pheromone level will also reduce as her fertility diminishes.
† Eggs laid in queen cup cells hatch after three days. As larvae, they're then fed for six days. Once their cells are sealed, the larvae mature for a further seven days before emerging as virgin queens.
‡ Any 'after swarms' or 'casts' behave differently: they travel higher, cover greater distances and are unlikely to be recovered.

the bees are only resting for an hour or two while several workers try to locate a suitable place to nest. As soon as returning scout bees have communicated their findings using the waggle dance,* the collective moves off once more to their new location. Worker honeybees that swarm are ready to draw new honeycomb at speed so that their queen can begin laying eggs again as soon as possible. If they can be swiftly contained within a standard box hive, the bees will therefore establish their prolific work for the well-prepared or perhaps fortuitous beekeeper.

While beekeeping itself is an ancient practice, the complex manner in which honeybees swarm and the crucial, associated detail of how they breed have only been understood for around 250 years. Although seldom acknowledged in contemporary accounts of apicultural history, Anton Janscha, the son of a beekeeper born in modern-day Slovenia, first described how bees breed in *Abhandlung von Schwärmen der Bienen* (*A Treaty on Bee Swarming*), 1771.†‎ What had previously been enshrouded in all manner of myth from mysticism to imperialism was accurately described by Janscha as a one-time 'nuptial' flight from the hive where the virgin queen mates with multiple partners – now considered to be anywhere between 10–20 drones – and returns to the hive with a distended abdomen along with the remains of drone bee genitalia. Importantly, Janscha connected honeybee breeding with swarming, as only a colony in the stage of producing virgin queens releases a primary swarm with the mature queen. Janscha noted that swarming was the

* the figure of eight communication, described by 1973 Nobel Prize winning Karl von Frisch, that honeybees ordinarily use to relay information about the location of plentiful forage sources

† Janscha worked at the Viennese Augarten under the provision for agricultural development during Empress Maria Theresa's reign of the Habsburg Empire. The Swiss naturalist, François Huber, is more commonly credited with the first accurate description of honeybee swarming and mating, even though he undertook his experiments on the subject from 1787–8 and published *Nouvelles Observations sur les Abeilles* (*New Observations on the Natural History of Bees*) in 1792.

multiplication of two colonies from one, enabling a hive to at least double its proliferation. He was particularly aided in his research by knowledge of the traditional hiving techniques used in his home region. In Upper Carniola, beekeepers had been keeping bees in wooden panel boxes known as *kranjici* since at least the mid-17th century,* enabling them to keep colonies year-on-year. *Kranjici*, stacked together and built into a house-like apiary accessible from the rear for ease of maintenance and honey harvesting, surpassed the standard woven, dome-shaped skep beehives most European beekeepers were still using in the 18th century. In order to access honey at harvest time, those that used skeps killed their bees by burning sulphur under hives, whereas *kranjic* users could harvest honey and retain their bees for the following year. Almost a century after Janscha's publication, in a treaty of similar scope, T. Wildman was appealing to skep users when he wrote:

> Were we to kill a hen for her egg, the cow for her milk, or the sheep for the fleece it bears, everyone would instantly see how much we should act contrary to our own interests; and yet this is practiced every year, in our inhuman and impolitic slaughter of the bees.[2]

The *kranjic* had long been advocated by Janscha as a more humane hiving system that also provided greater efficiency and control.

Without this focus on maintaining colonies year-on-year and annually monitoring swarming, little could have been done to develop honeybee breeding and queen rearing. What began as swarm collection incrementally progressed to more convenient means for beekeepers to maintain and increase hive numbers. As swarms are not always easy to retain, beekeepers have commonly

---

* An early account of *kranjici* was written in the 1689 publication by Janez Vajkard Valvasor, *Die Ehre der Herzogtums Krain* (*The Duchy of Carniola's Honour*).

turned towards suppressing their development instead. Today, for example, beekeepers intervene in the hive by removing queen cup cells as they appear* or by stealthily increasing hive space in order to alleviate crowding and encourage a coherent colony. For those who want to prevent colony proliferation and yet generate more colonies from their own stock, various methods exist to produce artificial swarms by splitting a colony in two before it would divide naturally. As most modern beekeepers would rather have stable colonies than deal with regular swarming, it's also common for hives to be re-queened annually even though queens can remain fertile for up to four years.† Rather than colonies naturally subdividing and perpetually reinforcing their species' swarming characteristics, honeybees have been bred to curb their propensity to swarm by increasing the queen bee's level of fertility. Obtaining reliably mated queen bees has therefore become central to contemporary beekeeping. Controlled environments are used to ensure that bees can be selectively reproduced. One approach is to *breed* bees by crossing honeybee subspecies, which with modern methods can be performed using artificial insemination in order to be assured a certain genetic combination for colonies. Another is to use selected breeder queens and *rear* new queens locally at remote sites that guarantee only drones and virgin queens released into these areas will mate there. The mountainous and forested environment of Upper Carniola in Slovenia, for example, provides ideally isolated areas for the controlled rearing of one of the most popular subspecies of honeybee worldwide: *Apis mellifera carnica*. As carniolans are renowned for their docility and high honey-yielding colonies, a large percentage of beekeepers worldwide keep *Apis mellifera carnica* rather than a subspecies that may have once been indigenous to their region. The potential for meeting European beekeepers with

* As seen when Edwin Clark was inspecting a hive in Lincolnshire, UK.
† Whether re-queening annually or maintaining queens for longer, beekeepers need to remain vigilant when colonies are increasing in size in order to retain fertile queens.

carniolan bees working their hives, for example, is so high that it was no surprise to see one German beekeeper in the Rheinland lifting a frame out of one of his hives and stroking the backs of his bees while remarking on how docile his carniolans were. The carniolan bee named after its origin within the Carniolan Alps – referred to as *kranjska* in Slovenia, *krainer* across the border in Carinthia, Austria, and *carniche* in Carnia, Italy – is specifically suited to a region with longer, colder winters, which produces small honeybee clusters that rapidly increase in size with the arrival of a temperate spring.

Bee-rearing Station
Upper Carniola, Slovenia

It's the height of the foraging season and a tired yet vivid turquoise pick-up truck loaded with active beehives stands stationary, its next journey a seemingly distant intention never to be realised. To the passing eye the truck resembles a traditional apiary, a *cebelnjak*, stacked with *kranjici*; Upper Carniola is definitely the place to come for remaining hints of long-held apicultural traditions and a landscape in which bees have thrived. In nearby Kranj, cornfields that overwhelm the scenery with multiple, long, thin lines are soon themselves overtaken by the forest that ultimately dominates over half of Slovenia. Azure lakes, glimpsed through trees, appear like crystal even without prior knowledge of their delicate mineral filtration. Rivers, winding their way through valleys, are cradled by the gorges they've channelled. Rich tapestries of mixed-forest mountainsides look as if they might capture the myth of an unmediated landscape from our distant past rather than tell a story of more recent change. Exploring further reveals that some communities raised in the mountains continue to work the land here, despite the limitations imposed by geography. Houses with vegetable gardens pitched on any small promontory are still lived in and being well tended. Although conjuring up such a rural idyll may be as much in the tone of my words as it is in their hands, I'm

reassured that this part of Upper Carniola is already oft-quoted as one of the most beautiful areas of Europe.

A multitude of small-scale apiaries collectively make Slovenia one of the most densely honeybee-populated areas of Europe.[3] In this region, beehives painted in cheerful, egalitarian colours, which strike resounding notes in wild flower meadows, have mostly replaced the hand-drawn character of older *kranjici* that were once prevalent here. Playfully and naïvely painted panels that depict a rural past influenced by a medley of ritual, superstition and religion are now collectors' items; captivating examples are reserved in vitrines at the apicultural museum in nearby Radovljica. Only occasional panels now remain outdoors in small towns renowned for beekeeping. One such apiary stands in Breznica, Zirovnica, at the foot of the Karavanke mountains, as a memorial to Anton Janscha: the hives, even with no bees animating their entrances, enliven the garden of Janscha's childhood home with a multitude of scenes. Images like that of a brown bear in profile, standing upright in white clerical robes, extending a prayer book and sharp, blood-red tongue, gently mock authority as was. In one of few panel images depicting beekeeping itself, a resting honeybee swarm is being collected into a box from a tree: *kranjici* buzzing with bees painted onto a *kranjic* is a fine illustration of the practical skill that Janscha proudly carried into his academic study.

The booklet I'm holding that brought me to this memorial also mentions the local bee-rearing stations, one of which is named after Janscha. Back on the main road, one of many turns eventually promises to lead resolutely away from the well-signed lure of Lake Bled and towards my destination. The description I'm using may not have been intended as directions but with some creative interpretation it seems to be bearing up: the nearby villages have long since faded from sight and the route that meanders its way towards and into the forest looks rarely used. As the track comes to its final conclusion, a neat sign pointing off to the left is a small yet definite indication of the bee-rearing station.

Any sense of the area's broader geography is immediately subdued by wandering through dense trees. With no fence or other demarcation to distinguish this site from its surroundings, it soon becomes apparent that the station is no more nor less than a tranquil area of the forest.

Under the canopy of beech, I suddenly spot a series of compact, colourful boxes planted somewhat haphazardly on stands along the inclining bank of steep ground. Each box, despite being numbered and tagged with a label noting when and how it has been monitored, looks more like a playschool object than a scientific tool kit. The boxes, constructed to house a small colony of worker honeybees and a newly hatched virgin queen, are known as mating nuclei. Over a period of 2–3 weeks, virgin queens at the site freely leave their containers to mate in flight with drones from colonies also pre-selected and located in the area by the station's organisers. This site, like other mating sites within Slovenia, has been chosen for its remote location at altitude away from farming and other honeybee colonies.

The location of the bee-rearing station, chosen to compliment the needs of carniolan bees, also looks like it would suit many a dedicated beekeeper.* Alongside the boxes, a simple, well-built house with a wood store, rain trap and solar water heater provides the means for a small team of people to live and work near the bees. The station, initiated in 2003 as a cross-border project between two beekeeping associations – one in Carinthia, the other in Upper Carniola – was realised in 2005 with regional and EU funding, and after a recent rest period is being used once more as a local resource. Beekeepers from regional associations benefit from the availability of queens to restock their hives that have been exclusively reared within the habitat in which they will raise colonies, rather than being imported from elsewhere.

* In fact, as I later learnt, the facility had until recently been largely run by one dedicated beekeeper in particular who managed the station until the age of 95.

Although I have questions about the international supply of carniolan bees, my first glimpse of honeybee rearing is unexpectedly small-scale and local. Any preconceived ideas I might have entertained that this process need be intensive have been challenged by this fine example of a practice that maintains regional carniolan variation.

Forested areas within the Slovenian Julian Alps, such as those near Breznica, are representative of environments where the honeybee has evolved subspecies distinctions. The European honeybee is considered to have migrated from Africa early in its evolution and established a rich variety of subspecies, as classified within the extensive morphological study by Friedrich Ruttner in 1978:

> The species *Apis mellifera* L. has a quite unusually large area of distribution. It extends from Southern Scandinavia in the North to the Cape of Good Hope in the South, from Dakar in the West to the Urals, Mashad and to the coast of Oman in the East. It was experimentally shown that it is in fact a single species, as all the different types from this enormous region, comprising the whole western part of the Old World, interbreed with full fertility. It is evident that the different types originated by geographic isolation and ecological adaptations.[4]

Although figures vary, it is generally considered that 28 subspecies have evolved within Europe's broad range of habitats.* In particular, the continent's geographically separate areas are thought to have isolated these different types to produce regional adaptation, as noted by Pilar De la Rúa, Rodolfo Jaffé, Raffaele

* Ruttner originally identified 24 subspecies. It's now agreed that 26 definitely exist and, in total, 28 are supposed.

Dall'Olio, Irene Muñoz and José Serrano in their 2009 paper on honeybee conservation:

> The present distribution of European honeybee subspecies has also been influenced by their location just after the Last Glacial Maximum (LGM), when the mountain chains of the Pyrenees, the Alps and the Balkans acted as geographical barriers in maintaining the isolation of populations.[5]

Subspecies *Apis mellifera mellifera* in the northwest (otherwise known as the dark European or German black bee) and *Apis mellifera carnica* in the Balkans (also known as the grey bee) were separated by ice and grew more distinct, as did *Apis mellifera ligustica*, a naturally cross-bred subspecies of the northern black bee and southern grey bee (commonly known as the Italian bee), that was further isolated south of the Alps. Subspecies evolution made distinct through distance and geographical boundaries over millennia has been dramatically interrupted by the regular, long-distance transportation of honeybees, however.

At Radovljica's apiculture museum (near the bee-rearing station), myriad artefacts chronicle regional apicultural developments, including intriguing displays of early commercial honeybee businesses. One display of particular note focuses on the aptly named Mihael Ambrozic who was the first beekeeper from Upper Carniola to trade bees worldwide with an export business he started in 1872 that went on to transport over 70,000 colonies. Although a relatively small-scale operation in comparison with today's export market, Ambrovic's business was remarkable for the extent of its reach at the time, which was made possible by the *kranjic*. In describing the application of this local system, De la Rúa et al. state:

... small Carinthian hives, traditionally employed
by beekeepers in the Austrian-Slovenian border,
facilitated the transport of *A. m. carnica* bees
outside their natural range.[6]

In this part of the world, beekeepers had been adapting the honeybee's natural propensity for nesting in dark tree trunk cavities into more convenient wooden boxes for centuries, and stacks of box hives were a small step away from the needs of convenient transportation hives. Under a series of historical world maps on display at the museum that pinpoint with proud silver indents the export of carniolan bees to locations as distant as Sydney and San Francisco, a seemingly ad hoc pile of boxes, as much packing cases as modern beehives, illustrate the means by which Jan Strgar transported colonies from 1903 onwards. After only seven years of operation, Ambrozic's young entrepreneurial successor had built a carniolan bee export business that was so successful he was able to open Slovenia's first commercial queen-rearing facility, which further streamlined his business into an international export operation. Across Europe, for example, trade was strong both within the Austro-Hungarian Empire and Germany, but also with the Russian Empire, Sweden, Norway, Denmark (including Iceland), the Netherlands, Belgium, Switzerland, Serbia, Greece and the UK. Business, meanwhile, was minimal with France and Spain, and non-existent with the Ottoman Empire (across Turkey), Bulgaria and throughout Italy. Where trade was open, beekeepers were keen to import 'exotic' subspecies, such as the carniolan. In areas where exchange was minimised or trade politically difficult, other subspecies, such as *Apis mellifera anatolica* in Turkic regions, remained isolated during this period. While *Apis mellifera ligustica* therefore remained distinct in Italy at this time, the Italian bee had also become a ready export and was as common if not more widespread than the carniolan bee across Europe and the rest of the world. Over a relatively short period of time, the ever increasing transportation of honeybee subspecies had in effect overridden the otherwise expansive evolutionary development of *Apis mellifera*. The benefits of evolution that allow the more incremental adaptation of ecotypes had been compromised.

Conversely, in order to maintain the evolutionary traits of honeybees we consider most desirable, breeders began preserving characteristics that distinguish certain subspecies. The typical grey abdomen that gives the carniolan its more common name has therefore become imperative, because it's an easily recognisable distinction between *Apis mellifera carnica* and its near relation *Apis mellifera ligustica*; a vibrant yellow stripe or two on the carniolan's abdomen is a likely sign that its lineage includes genes from the Italian bee's telltale warmer colouring. Where the carniolan bee has adapted to the demands of mountainous environments in Austria, Slovenia and the Balkans, the Italian subspecies has meanwhile adjusted to temperate climates with colonies that develop slowly in the spring. As a result, any interbreeding between *ligustica* and *carnica* may disadvantage colonies that ought to be resilient to extremes within their environment. Both the carniolan and the Italian honeybee have been reared and exported for their docility, ability to produce high honey yields and for their disease resistance, and yet any interbreeding undermines their value as commodities.

During the rise of honeybee trading, the UK imported both these subspecies and may have indeed benefited from their resistance when, for example, a virulent disease eradicated many of Britain's indigenous black bees. In 1906, the disease, initially known as the Isle of Wight Disease (as detailed in chapter one), decimated a huge number of colonies and yet left much of the imported Italian stock relatively unscathed. The greater survival rate of a non-native subspecies during successive bouts of the disease supported the notion that it was more resistant than native *Apis mellifera mellifera*. However, disease resistance is often the result of adaptation and it's possible that imported colonies may have also in some way carried and transmitted the catalysts of this disease.

At the time, faced with a failing apiary wrought by disease, one beekeeper in England turned his attention to breeding a more disease resistant bee. In 1917, Karl Kehrle from Germany, better known as Brother Adam of Buckfast Abbey, began breeding the Buckfast bee based on principles of crossing pure strains of honeybee subspecies. In order to source suitable bees for his programme, Brother Adam travelled extensively throughout Europe, Africa and Asia. His breeding work then took place at isolated locations on Dartmoor. The combination of extensive journeying and ongoing selection eventually resulted in what we now know as the Buckfast bee containing genetic stock from *Apis mellifera ligustica*, *Apis mellifera mellifera* (English and French varieties), *Apis mellifera anatolica* (Turkish), *Apis mellifera cecropia* (Greek), and two rare, docile strains of African bee *Apis mellifera sahariensis* and *Apis mellifera monticola*. Having crossed different subspecies, Brother Adam was able to breed a bee that benefited from the vigour of hybridisation. Like other hybrid forms, however, the Buckfast bee was predestined to be genetically unpredictable beyond its first generation: virgins born of Buckfast queens are not guaranteed to produce the same desirable traits. As with pure strains, hybrid virgins may mate with drones of unspecified heritage and further interbreeding will then take place. In order to maintain breed integrity, those beekeepers who use Buckfast colonies therefore tend to re-queen their hives from breeders' stock.

Today, however, most UK colonies, unless recently imported,* now contain hybridised bees regardless of whether the beekeeper maintains Buckfast or not. The close proximity of

---

* For some beekeepers the lure of regularly importing subspecies for a potentially easily manageable (i.e. less aggressive) bee is still a strong compulsion.

hives encourages interbreeding between different subspecies that have been imported. As in many other locations across Europe, the international trade and breeding of honeybees has resulted in few areas maintaining what Brother Adam was initially searching for: pure strains of honeybee subspecies. The integrity of subspecies *Apis mellifera mellifera* in particular has been largely overwhelmed by more popular subspecies, which have in turn been assumed into hybridised forms. Many scientists are indeed concerned by the rate at which the honeybee is now becoming homogenised throughout Europe, as discussed by De la Rúa et al.:

> The intense dissemination of Italian and Carniolan honeybees throughout the European continent has resulted in the almost complete replacement of *A. m. mellifera* by *A. m. carnica* in central European countries such as Germany, and the hybridisation of all three subspecies in Scandinavian countries and the British Isles.[7]

They are noticing the broad introgression of a species due to reduced regional variation and therefore lower overall species diversity. Indeed, as the article continues:

> ... after finding little population differentiation in continental Italy, Dall'Olio et al. (2007) concluded that intensive queen breeding and migratory beekeeping have caused an amalgamation of local Italian Peninsula populations into a single gene pool.[8]

That the introgression of a subspecies is happening even before export is perhaps of most concern. Within the study conducted by Raffaele Dall'Olio and colleagues at the Istituto Nazionale di

Apicoltura (National Institute of Apiculture), Bologna, scientists specifically state that:

> As Italian environments show huge differences across the peninsula and islands, we were surprised not to have found specific ecotypes within *A. m. ligustica*. ... it currently looks as if the queen breeding routine ... has caused an amalgamation of local populations into one large Italian population.[9]

Critically, *ligustica* bees reared from breeder queens in Italy can no longer offer the genetic variation once prized from 'Old World' subspecies exports.

In the 'New World', the mass importation of honeybees and intensive breeding programmes appear to have conduced particularly low genetic diversity. DNA analysis produced in 1993, for example, which tested the genetic variation of colonies from 22 commercial apiaries in the south-east of the US found that "96% of colonies could trace their roots to Italy and the Balkans, from where races were imported in the 19th century".[10] When the US banned European imports with the 1922 Honeybee Act for fear of transporting the tracheal mite, *Acarapis woodii*,* the continent's source of pure honeybee strains was also suspended. The expansion of industrialised agriculture, especially after WWII in the US, encouraged such a dramatic increase of honeybee rearing and breeding that the sample 22 apiaries screened for data in 1993 "used just 308 breeder queens to produce almost half a million new queens for sale".[11]† A statistic such as this suggests that a phenomenal amount of virgin queens were born of each breeder that year alone. Considering that a colony produces only a few

* At that point, *Acarapis woodii* was considered the cause of the Isle of Wight or Acarine Disease.
† Half a million queens constituted one sixth of new stock at the time.

virgins to replace a mature queen, forcing so many virgins from one queen's eggs is a gross exaggeration of natural reproduction.

A decade later in 2004, when colony losses became prominent, the US government decided to partially lift this embargo on honeybee imports in order for beekeepers to quickly replace failing commercial stock and fulfil large pollination contracts. Aeroplanes full of honeybee colonies were then 'shipped in' to replenish American apiaries and, in this instance, new stock was imported from Australia where honeybee colonies are currently varroa-free. Unsurprisingly, these newly arrived colonies lasted no more than one season on their new continent: honeybee colonies from Australia that encountered varroa for the first time showed no resistance whatsoever to the parasite. Unfortunately, in their attempts to sustain commercial practices at any cost, some beekeepers became complicit in the death of immense quantities of honeybees; importing thousands of colonies from one continent into another for each pollination season is neither commercially viable nor sensitive to environmental differences. Over two centuries ago, we developed a more mutual, ongoing relationship with bees, progressing from poisoning colonies in order to extract honey to genuine *beekeeping.* If we've now returned to a situation where bees can only be maintained on a yearly basis, we have to admit that we're failing our apicultural tradition of honeybee and human co-existence.

The Australian government may now be attempting to secure the health of at least its internal colony stock by banning honeybee imports, as USA governors did 90 years ago, but this restriction can't protect the same bees from their own weakened genetic pool. A significant sector of honeybee farming in Australia, like the States, has developed into large-scale enterprise in order to service similarly large-scale pollination needs, and, unfortunately, these beekeepers are also increasingly dependent on honeybees with low genetic variation, as noted in 2010 by Benjamin and McCallum:

Queen breeding is carried out by a small number
of breeders. A 2007 survey of the genetic make-
up of commercial and feral honeybees in Western
Australia found similar results to the US. The
commercial populations were derived from the
Italian honeybee.[12]

While many species of wild bee are considered indigenous
to both North America and Australia, neither continent is
thought to have had honeybees prior to subspecies importation.
Although US and Australian colonisation occurred two
centuries apart,* the mass transportation of honeybees from
Europe commenced simultaneously in the late 19th century. As
neither continent shows any genetic trace of the first black bee
colonies transported from the UK, the genetic variation in both
world locations has been determined by the more recent arrivals
of popular subspecies from elsewhere in Europe. In Australia,
the existence of feral colonies – some of which may even be
descendant from 'early' colonisation[13]† – gives some hope for

* Honeybees arrived on both continents onboard ships in
skep beehives from the UK. During the 17th century, pilgrims
who famously travelled by boat and colonised North America
established the first western honeybee subspecies across the
Atlantic. A letter sent from the Virginia Company in London
to the governor and councillor in Virginia, USA, dated 5th
December 1621, mentions "divers sorte of seed, and fruit trees
... and beehives" carried on the ship Discovery, which left
England in November on a four month journey to the 'New
World'. Honeybees were first successfully imported in Australia
in 1822 on a missionary ship carrying convicts from the UK. The
transport of black bees was especially remarkable for the extent of
the journey with livestock that lasted a whole five-months.
† A recent study of honeybee genetics in Western Australia has
identified feral bees with haplotypes originating from *Apis
mellifera iberica*, the honeybee native to Spain and France, which
may have been initially transported to Australia by Spanish
missionaries.

the eventual long-term adaptation of *Apis mellifera* subspecies to the continent. At present, the difficulty of such a process is eased by there being less honeybee disease in Australia. However, it's worth emphasising that, despite the US's ban on imports, all of the parasites and pathogens it was feared would be transported to the continent arrived in due course, including varroa that destroyed all feral honeybee colonies during the late 1980s into the 1990s.[14] Unlike other livestock, insects have a canny way of passing border controls unseen and there may be no clear way of assuring the 100% restricted entry of a honeybee where it's not wanted.

Despite various import embargoes, the global trade of honeybees hasn't been thoroughly legislated to date. The international export of queen bees and even full honeybee colonies is undertaken regularly but with minimal restrictions. Being neither mammal, bird nor fish, the honeybee falls outside standard livestock classification and we appear to have missed the significance of allowing the near open trade of a farmed insect that we can only partially contain and control. The EU, for example, allows the distribution of honeybees without consideration of subspecies suitability, as stated by De la Rúa et al.:

> EU beekeeping legislation has not always been consistent regarding the preservation of honeybee biodiversity; the use of local races has been encouraged in the past (EU Regulation 1804/99) but honeybee trading without any race constraint or inspection is currently allowed if sanitary certificates are provided (Decision 2003/881/ EC).[15]

Sanitary practices are of course a necessary part of good beekeeping husbandry but they don't determine whether a colony or queen bee is an appropriate subspecies for an area.

Even if a non-native bee might then have slowly adapted to its new environment, ongoing honeybee importation interrupts this process. Trading popular European honeybee subspecies worldwide has arguably impacted our largest effect on the honeybee, and yet through this transportation we've paradoxically relinquished most responsibility, and with it control, for the species. It's common for beekeepers to receive parcels through the post, each containing a mated queen alongside a small cohort of worker bees, all primed and ready to contribute new brood to colonies. Whilst in transit, these bees mirror the lack of ownership of a swarm in flight.

Although beekeeping is ordinarily a highly conscientious practice, the ease of global honeybee trading has influenced the accepted perception that desirable species traits can be prioritised over local subspecies adaptation. Fortunately, in certain areas of Europe, where subspecies haven't yet been significantly imported, regional adaptation still exists. As 'indigenous' subspecies are increasingly appreciated for their environmental as well as economic value, beekeepers are therefore increasingly looking to areas such as Upper Carniola in Slovenia for example of good breeding and rearing practices.

Aleš Gregorc
Professor and researcher of honeybee rearing
Agricultural Institute of Slovenia,
Ljubljana, Slovenia

The large-scale yet reassuringly local map dominating the main wall in Aleš Gregorc's office, liberally tagged with a multitude of little white markers, is intriguingly difficult to read. As Aleš passes his hand across 'Slovenia', the pieces of paper gently animate until he rests on one area in particular. The label indicates a forest in the Bellakrajina region; I'm told this is where Slovenia's most recently established rearing station is located. Work has been underway since 2010 to prepare the area, so that beekeepers can conserve the region's carniolan variation there. Aleš hopes that with more funds the project can continue in line with the work already established in other areas of Slovenia.

In total, Aleš and his colleagues at the institute supervise the work of 30–35 official honeybee experts operating 30 mating sites for beekeeping associations across Slovenia. The institute receives some of its finance from beekeeping associations that require its support and guidance to operate funded projects. Advice, monitoring and research are then provided by the institute to help maintain the quality of practices at rearing stations and by association members. One project at the institute undertaken from 2006 to 2010, for example, involved the analysis of queen samples from rearing stations and included one morphological study in particular that identified the weight of queens, the weight of their ovaries, any pathogens they were carrying (including nosema fungal infections), the amount of sperm they store, and their distribution of internal tubes within ovaries. Notably, this research focused on the reproductive health of carniolan queens. Additional research, which also culminated in 2010, identified the selection criteria for queens and the minimum requirement necessary for apiaries to qualify for carniolan queen-rearing programmes. Colonies were tested for "gentleness, swarming behaviour, colony strength, racial characteristics,* honey production, extension of capped brood, hygienic behaviour and the presence of *Nosema* spp. [species] spores".[16] Importantly, the criteria identified not only desirable honeybee traits but also factors that determine regional variation and overall bee health in order to improve

* including abdominal colouration and Cubital index (an exacting measurement within wing length)

subspecies selection for population variability and the preservation of local adaptation.

As Aleš infers, one of the biggest discussions within apicultural circles at the moment is about ecotypes and Slovenia is already well placed to further advance honeybee biodiversity. Colonies in the country's Alpine regions, for example, where workers are adapted to foraging honeydew, are already distinct from flower foraging specialists of the north-west, despite being the same subspecies. The wealth of Carniola as a region is a subspecies heritage that has evolved over much longer than even Slovenia's oldest traditions can possibly compare. Regional beekeepers are now even being encouraged to name their services after the area in which they work or under the name of the farm or station where their queens are reared; the collective aim is to determine colonies by location and move away from automatically associating them with pure racial characteristics. This highly commendable practice is possible, and indeed funded, because Slovenian beekeepers are already in a very privileged position: they're able to focus on queen rearing from locally-adapted breeder queens.

In certain beekeeping circles, local queen rearing is increasingly considered preferable to breeding specifically for desirable traits. This approach to rearing promotes genetic continuation rather than developing more contrived variation and supports the adaptation of a subspecies to its environment. Most beekeepers in Slovenia continue to use mating sites, so that their practice is as close to the honeybee's natural habit and habitat as possible. Selected drones and virgin queens are located in designated sites and mate in flight. This process parallels other farming practice and is no different in principle, for example, to keeping a designated ram and ewes to maintain a flock of specifically reared sheep. This controlled natural process is an interesting notion, however, and of course involves the selection of what is considered to be the strongest specimens for rearing.

I'm therefore keen to know from Aleš whether he considers any rearing practices could be disadvantageous to bee health. He immediately acknowledges that any intervention to colony life is potentially detrimental. It is known, for example, that colonies prefer to work uninterrupted inside hives that simulate the dark spaces where they would naturally choose to nest and that disturbing bees too often can weaken colonies. In relation to rearing stations in particular, the mating nuclei used are one step further removed from normal colony practice and so the containment of virgin queens and their small working colonies shouldn't be down-sized too far: research at the institute has ascertained that if nuclei are too small, queen bee health can be threatened by higher levels of nosema.

Aleš tells me that in order to improve their chances of maintaining healthy colonies, some beekeepers in Slovenia minimise their involvement in rearing to an even greater extent. Not all mating sites, for example, use pre-selected drones and very few Slovenian beekeepers are presently moving their practice towards the other extreme: artificial insemination. Although certain scientists at the Agricultural Institute of Slovenia and local beekeepers have experience of insemination techniques, few choose to utilise their skill: only 50–100 queens per year are artificially inseminated at the institute. The process is considered labour intensive and less necessary given the environmental possibilities for rearing in Slovenia. I suggest that the process might also be less culturally acceptable, but Aleš counters that 50–70,000 queens are artificially inseminated annually in Catholic Poland, where greater social offence could be imagined. There, industrial agriculture and a lack of isolated habitats have proven more important.

In landscapes where it's still possible to establish isolated mating sites, it would seem that rearing in this way self-regulates itself as a small-scale enterprise of greater benefit to bee health and genetic variation. On average, official Slovenian rearers produce 1,000 queens with the largest operation producing no more than 2,500 fertilised queens per year. Queens are then distributed among beekeepers from local associations. Many beekeepers subsequently maintain colonies within the area where they were reared. Although Slovenia is a relatively small country, those beekeepers who then transport their colonies to different sites likely travel further than the direct environ to which their bees are adapted and so may disturb the balance of these precise adaptations. Honeybee transportation within Slovenia is consequently a fervent topic for scientists and beekeepers in relation to maintaining biodiversity. One of the institute's funding strands from the EU relates to the preservation of colonies in Slovenia and is critically linked to honeybee transportation. Beekeepers who have always moved hives to increase the productivity of their bees are now under pressure, perhaps for the first time, to consider that some of their standard methods to promote large honey-yielding colonies may be contrary to good practice.

Another economically driven practice of even greater impact to genetic diversity is still encouraged in Slovenia, however: honeybee export. As there's still a strong, global marketplace for carniolan bees, the government supports beekeepers with queen export businesses who can profit regularly from the international sale of *Apis mellifera carnica*. The beekeeper who produces the most queens in Slovenia, for example, exports to countries such as Denmark and Japan. Bees are also often sold to the UK and Germany. The carniolan is even knowingly exported to beekeepers choosing to breed *Apis mellifera carnica* with *Apis mellifera ligustica* in an attempt to gain benefit from a mix of the two subspecies characteristics. At this point, care of genetic adaption has obviously become redundant. For the good work being undertaken to preserve the suitability and genetic variation of *Apis mellifera carnica* to be successful there needs to be a global solution to bee rearing.

Encouragingly, a recently initiated international programme does exist that aims to coordinate the work of different beekeeping communities and scientific institutes. Coloss, an organisation of scientists, beekeepers and industry members from 55 countries, is producing the 'Bee Book' which aims to present sustainable strategies to combat colony losses. Aleš is part of the Coloss working group dedicated to bee-breeding research that currently contains representatives from Germany, Austria, Croatia, Hungary, Slovakia, the Czech Republic, Slovenia and Italy. Within this group, representatives from areas where subspecies *Apis mellifera ligustica* and *Apis mellifera carnica* have evolved are significantly present. The organisation as a whole also includes members from Africa (Algeria, South Africa), the Middle East (Iran, Israel, Sudan, Jordan, Egypt, Kyrgystan, Kyrgyz Republic), the Far East (Thailand, China, Japan) and the Americas (Argentina, Uruguay, Mexico, Chile, Colombia, Venezuala, Peru, Brazil, USA and Canada). With co-ordinated representation from across the globe comes hope of universal honeybee re-diversification.

Aleš' enthusiasm for solutions is based on something very close to home. As we look back at the map, simultaneously expanded and refined by our discussion, he points to a very specific area in the Julian Alps, which once more focuses our conversation to a local perspective. Aleš' hand this time indicates the location of 40–50 colonies on a mountain plateau, his own apiary, which he only moves annually into the nearby valley for winter. With 20 years experience as an apiculturist and even more as a beekeeper, Aleš partially sees the future of beekeeping within education. He expects a return to greater farming knowledge, not less, and from this shared perspective of high aspiration I hope he's right. To see beekeeping and honeybee rearing live on at a local level and in a more genetically adapted form would perhaps be the most rewarding outcome of all.

four

Far from fields and meadows, a ruby lattice of stems and a snow-white web of silken threads captivate swathes of foreground scenery. The notably wild rather than cultivated flowering plant, rosebay willowherb or fireweed, grows especially well here towards the Arctic Circle. In nearby forests, spruce trees reach with long, slow, intermittent progress for heights gained far quicker further south, while complementary wild blueberries and the lesser-known orange cloudberries lie conspicuously bountiful within a soft, silvery-grey bed of lichen. This visually delicate yet robust forest floor, undulating over rock and fallen tree, subtly disguises an under course of swamp water, which in summer breeds voracious mosquitoes that far outnumber human inhabitants. Travelling along the well-maintained roadways connecting distant houses and villages, you're more likely to see reindeer crossing or come across the telltale signs of bears who've left berry-stained markers rather than encounter another set of tyres rolling by. In fact, if it weren't for the roads, this area would come close to the image often conjured of Scandinavian wilderness.

North Sweden, bordered by Norway and the Scandinavian Mountain Chain to the west and by Finland and the Gulf of Bothnia to the east, provides one of Europe's more extreme biomes. Its proximity to both the Arctic and the Gulf Stream causes a specific set of climatic circumstances. Snow can cover the land for over eight months of the year and little to no sun appears in winter. At the other end of the seasonal orbit, days are long with midnight sun and sequential white nights persist without sunset. The growing season is therefore a short, intense period of time which leaves North Sweden inhospitable to many of the plants and animals commonly used in conventional European farming. As a result, Sweden's agriculture and indeed population are principally concentrated in the south of the country. For honeybees that need adequate time to complete their cycle of colony development before winter, this extreme environment would seemingly present a stark challenge. Whereas temperate climates provide at least six months for colonies to forage, only three months are reliably warm enough near the Arctic. Given the current pressures on the honeybee in general, who might then consider keeping hives here where other forms of agriculture are conspicuously absent?

Helen Bergqvist
Regional beekeeping expert, Lapland, Sweden

I'm driving south preoccupied with winter's arrival having just seen the first snow further north. The slender silver birch trees I notice out of the corner of my eye are laying claim to the only cascade here though, their golden autumnal leaves already on the ground. It's their distinctive trunks that form a white border and visual rhythm between a herd of sheep and that row of painted beehives over there. In the time it takes to stop, step out and gently adjust to this great outdoors, a young woman appears from the adjacent farmhouse. I start a conversation and Mia explains that her hives are relatively new and so considers she has little experience to impart about remote beekeeping in the north. Everything she does know, however, has been learnt from a local expert who I should visit to find out more. Although Mia can't reach Helen Bergqvist on the phone, she thinks it's worth heading over to her house anyway: it'll be simple, she says, just keep an eye out for more beehives.

Travelling off-map down a well-worn track, with a confidence that transforms what had been a slow lope of a journey into an excitable quest, ultimately reveals Helen's village, which even after several passes falls several beehives short of success. With few houses lining the road, it's fortuitous that two people happen to be unloading a car, and a brief introduction to the story so far means they can reassure me that this is the right place and that Helen is at this very moment on her way back from the 'summerhouse'. Despite such a remote environment with so many miles between people, it's becoming clear that neighbourliness doesn't rely on proximity here in Västerbotten.

When Helen arrives, she approaches as if meeting a long-lost friend that I now have the potential to become. Immediately there's an invitation to her house, only a short distance away, to see her colonies. It turns out that Helen's beehives, some made of wood and others of plastic, are now hidden behind the house alongside the wall of a spacious outbuilding. Inside, Helen stores a wealth of beekeeping equipment for hive maintenance, honey extraction and packaging, which is systematically organised for a small honey production business to function efficiently. With a flurry, it's explained that there are more jars than normal because last year Helen's colonies exceeded their usual honey yield by an extraordinary amount: whereas an average year returns around 225–250kg (496–551lbs), in 2008 she extracted a colossal 700kg (1,543lbs). Her honey, which has become especially popular with certain affluent buyers in Norway, makes good profit.

As we talk more, Helen becomes intrigued by the contrasting story I share from beekeepers I'd met in Finland whose apiary located at a similar latitude has experienced consecutive annual down-turns in productivity. The weather having been optimum for bees last year suggests to Helen that other factors must have affected their yields and, with some urgency, takes this as her cue to show me some relevant data. Searching amongst the leather and wool work in her office-come-studio, Helen finds what she's carefully filed away: a map which, although only printed on a piece of A4 ink-jet paper, communicates a lot with remarkably little. The colourful orange, yellow and blue representation of Sweden is valuable because it depicts the varroa parasite's spread across the country and includes one special area that remains conspicuously blank. The map's orange sections, highlighting southern Sweden and the border with Finland, constitute the largest collective area and represent the country's greatest infestation. Varroa, it would seem, arrived in Sweden from three distinct directions: while two areas characterised by higher population densities and transport connections probably imported the parasite from Central Europe, a third route occurred over land in the north from Finland. Next to the orange sections, yellow and then blue-coloured regions, denoting lower intensity infestation, clearly show the parasite's further movement and development from colony to colony. Meanwhile, the uncoloured area of the map in the north with its back to the mountains is of greatest interest: it's the first evidence I've seen of a varroa-free region in Europe and am surprised its status isn't more well-known. Although Helen's honeybees haven't as yet been infected with varroa, she lives on the edge of the map's lower ominous blue area which suggests the inevitable fate of her colonies. Helen, who's involved in the local co-ordination of a varroa-detection programme, passes me the map with both pride and an element of resignation. The map is bound to look different in a few years time; both Helen and I know that all Swedish hives are likely to succumb in due course to the same malaise as neighbouring Finland.

Perhaps to sweeten the note of this map in my hands, Helen also gives me a presentation package of honey. As we're standing by the front door, the elaborately wrapped jar of light, creamy produce topped with a smaller complement of eucalyptus-flavoured honey feels like a parting gift, and yet, all of a sudden, a natural moment to leave transforms into an invitation to visit the summerhouse. Despite having only just packed up and left, Helen says we should definitely go. It's not far and there are more beehives that have been placed there as a wintertime experiment. It would be a great opportunity to learn more about why this area of Sweden is so good for bees. With the enthusiasm of one who knows the high season is almost over, Helen then hurriedly packs a basket of provisions before the door to the 'winterhouse' resolutely closes behind us.

We may have travelled only a dozen kilometres from the house in the village but when we arrive on the banks of the Långseleån river our location feels deeply distinctive from what was already remote rural life. Having woven our way along an intricate woodland track, we pass into an open glade dotted with wooden buildings of varying size and purpose. Helen and her husband have slowly built upon her family's settlement and are in the process of making a traditional eight-sided outhouse hewn from whole tree trunks to sit alongside the main wooden-clad housing. Later I learn that one of the nearby sheds is a sauna and another contains the family's collection of agricultural tools, justifiably known as 'the museum'. Completing the picture are three hives, also wooden, that have been placed carefully alongside the water's edge. Everything appears to be in its right and just place.

Helen is understandably proud of her heritage which extends into an in-depth knowledge of her environment. Prompted by the plant specimens collected by her grandchildren for botanical study that remain on the kitchen table, Helen begins to discuss the local flora she knows benefits her honeybee colonies. While sipping tea flavoured with pale, intensely-sweet honey, we pore over sumptuous images of wild flowers from a floral identification book. Using Latin names as a common frame of reference, Helen pinpoints a diverse range of flowers she knows her bees forage, pausing here and there for greater emphasis on plants such as *Epilobium*. The spearhead of purple flowers, unrecognisable to me in their summer guise as the billows of fireweed I've seen everywhere within the surrounding countryside, are what largely give this local honey its distinctive colour and flavour. Helen's honeybees forage almost exclusively from wild plants; other than small-scale gardening, such as the few fruit bushes and vegetables in the plot outside, there's no horticulture in the local area.

The following morning, standing in the garden beside Helen's rose bushes generously dressed with hips, there's one last opportunity to sample some more of her bees' work before ultimately saying farewell with a warmth equal to that of my welcome. As the riverside gate opens, I imagine their keeper finishing hive preparations for the coming winter. This year Helen is encasing her hives in layers of polystyrene to further protect clusters of bees against sub-zero temperatures; the artificial purity and clean lines of the white plastic cases will remain conspicuous within their environment only until the first snowfall arrives to soften and eventually bury all edges.

—

Beekeepers, especially those in the far north, know winter is one of the greatest challenges to the survival of their bees. As honeybees need to maintain a central hive temperature of around 35°C,* in Västerbotten, where winters averagely dip to -15°C and can fall to as low as -30°C, beekeepers and their colonies need to take care during this 'down-time'. That apiculture can succeed in an environment this demanding is testament to the skill of dedicated beekeepers. That colonies can withstand the rigours of such a harsh climate is also testament to the extraordinary resilience of the honeybee.

While it's already astounding that colonies can survive in this region, the fact that they're currently so healthily-adjusted and productive here is all the more exceptional. Although summers are short, high-quality, copious honey is a standout characteristic of Swedish beekeeping; when discussing honey yields with Aleš Gregorc at the Slovenian Institute, for example, he admired the apparent ease with which Swedish beekeepers could rapidly collect quantities of honey in comparison with trickling Upper Carniolan mountain harvests. As honeybees are predisposed to

* In winter, honeybees achieve a constant temperature by vibrating in their cluster and share this work by rotating positions.

work whenever conditions are optimum, they can collectively make foraging flights round the clock without end over long Scandinavian summer days. What would have taken six months further south can therefore occur within an intensive three-month period in North Sweden. Low hive density additionally minimises the spread of parasites such as varroa and, with little disease to hinder colonies, there's even greater opportunity for honeybees to maximise this intensive period of development. The benefits of wild plants rather than crops may be more directly advantageous to bees than humans, but the absence of other farming reduces the likelihood of agricultural chemicals contaminating forage and otherwise negatively impacting honeybee physiognomy; that honeybees are succeeding in a relatively uncultivated environment is telling.

Helen's bumper honey harvest of 2008 is also an indication of the climatic changes that may be altering the balance of beekeeping. The mildest winter on record across most parts of Europe in 2007–8 undoubtedly improved the chances for Helen's honeybees to survive and, with fewer winter losses leading to stronger colony numbers in the summer, her bees tripled their honey yield. While one warm winter may have been remarkable, this phenomenon is becoming more common; higher overall temperatures are significantly reducing the impact of harsh winter conditions in North Sweden.*

In fact, while Scandinavian summers are warming, winter temperatures are increasing to such an extent that the northern Scandinavian biome is being radically altered by a reduction in snow, an increase in rain and the Arctic permafrost and glaciers melting. Recent analysis of ground temperatures collated from measurements within the subarctic region of Sweden between 1956

---

* Beekeepers always hope for an uninterrupted start to the honeybee foraging season so that colonies can find enough food at their most vulnerable time of year. Elsewhere in Europe, spring's early arrival has not always been advantageous: brief, uncharacteristic warm spells have often been followed by a return to cold weather, freezing and destroying the growth of early budding plants.

and 2006 outlines a marked increase in winter, spring and autumn temperatures.[1]* A Swedish government report published in 2007, based on similar data identifying rising temperatures throughout Sweden, states that:

> During the years 1991–2005, the average annual temperature was 1°C higher than in the period 1961–1990. The increase was at its clearest in the winter, at over 2°C in central and northern parts of the country.[2]

The report, which also includes predictive analysis of climate change in Sweden, suggests that Scandinavia will continue to experience above average temperature increases:

> Warming will not be evenly distributed around the world. It is expected to be considerably higher over the Arctic and the land masses of the northern hemisphere, with the Arctic experiencing around twice the global average.[3]

A significant section of the report is devoted to the anticipated impacts of climate change in relation to land use that largely reinforces the positive impact milder winters might have on Sweden's agricultural potential.† Honeybees often provide an early indication of environmental health and fertility, and in this case their strength signifies a potential rise in options for other forms of agriculture in Sweden. It's already recognised within

---

* Digital analysis of ground temperatures measured in two locations over a fifty year period in Abisko, Sweden, concludes that temperatures have risen on average by 0.3°C per decade in an area where less snow and higher air temperatures have also been systematically recorded.

† Should Scandinavia's ambient temperatures continue to increase, the range of crops farmers could grow would vastly develop agricultural potential in far northern Europe.

the report, however, that while "yields of autumn-sown crops will increase, and new crops may be introduced … problems with pests such as insects, fungi and viruses will increase in a warmer climate."[4] Although climate change may advance possibilities for agriculture and indeed beekeeping in North Sweden, the long-term ramifications of altered biomes across Scandinavia, such as increasingly frequent precipitation, will no doubt simultaneously bring untold challenges.

While significant amounts of rain would curtail honeybees foraging, a warmer environment would likely exacerbate a greater, well-known threat to bees: the varroa mite. In a 2010 article, outlining an expansive assessment of varroa's impact on honeybee colonies, scientists Yves Le Conte, Marion Ellis and Wolfgang Ritter state:

> Factors such as weather conditions, longer brood rearing periods and large amounts of drone brood can dramatically increase the mite population size. Global warming can induce longer spring and fall periods resulting in longer brood rearing periods and more drone brood, both of which lead to significantly larger mite population at the end of the year.[5]

Warmer temperatures are not only encouraging increased productivity and honeybee brood rearing, but also the multiplication of varroa. While climate change is improving the ability of honeybee colonies in Sweden to generally produce more honey, a significant number of beekeepers are concurrently reporting colonies infected with varroa that then die in winter. From 2009 to 2010, for example, 26% of Sweden's overall colony losses were definitively associated with varroa infestation.[6] So, although fewer colonies may perish from the usual stresses of intensely cold winters such as starvation and dysentery, the arrival of varroa along with larger honeybee colonies may ultimately result in greater colony losses. Varroa is certainly a serious problem for beekeepers, not least in Sweden.

One particularly ground breaking study aims to counter the increasing threat of varroa by utilising Sweden's low human and honeybee population densities. In 1999, on the island of Gotland in the Baltic Sea, scientists established the first stage of an investigation to evaluate the impact of reducing human intervention in the control of varroa-infested hives. By isolating colonies, they hoped to determine whether short-term adaptation could encourage a more balanced host-parasite co-habitation. The Gotland Bond Project, led by Ingemar Fries, established eight apiaries at the southernmost tip of the island with a total 150 hives all infested with an initially regulated number of *Varroa destructor* mites.* All hives were then left unmanaged but monitored four times a year for winter losses, bee population in the spring, swarming, and infestation rates in the autumn. After high mortality and low swarm rates midway through the initial experiment, there was then a strong correlation between lower honeybee mortality and increased swarming rates during the last two years of the experiment. By 2005, the amount of colonies may have significantly reduced to only 13 hives – five colonies from the original apiaries and eight from swarms – but the survival of even a few colonies after six years without any treatment was a promising outcome for the long-term adaptation of these two species, as Fries and his colleagues present in summary:

> Winter mortality rate decreased from 76% and 57% in the third and fourth years to 13% and 19% in the fifth and sixth years. Swarming rates increased from zero the third field season to 57.1% and 36.4% in the last two years ... Our data suggest that a host-parasite co-adaptation has occurred ensuring survival of both the host and the parasite.[7]

* 36–89 mites per colony

The results indicated that honeybees may develop resistance to varroa if allowed to swarm over a period of years.

After recording these outcomes on the island, scientists keen to develop the project's potential scope then extended the experiment onto the Swedish mainland. The survival of some colonies from the initial project encouraged the scientists to relocate varroa-tolerant queens from the island. In 2006, seven apiaries, each containing eight colonies derived from Bond Project stock and eight with control queens,* were established with minimal intervention† for an initial monitoring period of three years within set areas of grass and woodland. By 2008, four out of the seven apiaries were still operational and figures collated in 2007 and 2008 present a reduction in overall mite infestation levels for surviving colonies. Only one test colony in one apiary exceeded the infestation level of neighbouring control colonies, whereas the remaining resistant queens and their colonies returned favourable results in relation to their equivalent controls. Of the original 112, twelve remaining test colonies suggest that the reintroduction of more adaptive honeybee colonies into environments containing non-resistant colonies may also be possible.

Although identifying the exact cause of greater co-adaptation between bee and parasite is beyond the scope of the Bond Project, Fries and his team can confidently assert that certain beekeeping methods likely impair the development of varroa-tolerance:

> Our results allow us to conclude that the problems facing the apicultural industry with

* As with standard scientific practice, 'control' stock was used in this experiment so that results would include the progress of queens and colonies not reared on Gotland as a neutral comparison.

† A single treatment of the organic compound oxalic acid, which is being increasingly used as a less astringent treatment against varroa by many beekeepers, was introduced into the routine for both Bond and control colonies in October.

mite infestations probably is linked to the apicultural system, where beekeepers remove the selective pressure induced from the parasitism by removing mites through control efforts.[8]

The common practice of treating varroa-infected colonies with chemical preparations is becoming increasingly controversial, especially since varroa has developed resistance to compounds such as fluvalinate in Apistan and, as a result, is now harder to control. While colonies can weaken through the use of synthetic chemical treatments in the hive,[9] surviving mites become more resilient.[10] The search for means to control varroa is therefore now challenged by an even stronger and more virulent parasite. Sensibly, research is increasingly centred on non-toxic methods of control. Some beekeepers, for example, now remove drone brood when least harmful to colony development in order to reduce the potential number of mites that can fully gestate in the hive. Scientists in the US, Germany and the UK are meanwhile working on research and breeding programmes to encourage the hygienic behaviour already evident in honeybee colonies. The overarching aim of these studies, albeit using different methods, focuses on reducing varroa numbers to a tolerable level in the hive through the selection of bees pre-disposed to removing varroa infected brood.* In these instances, however, the control of varroa still centres on removing mites rather than allowing the honeybee to adapt and increase its tolerance. Fewer mites in any varroa-infested colony would nevertheless offer more time for the processes that enable co-adaptation to develop and stand a chance of succeeding.

---

* At a mid-point in their lifecycle, workers become 'cleaning' bees and remove anything unwanted from the hive, such as dead bees. It has been noted that some cleaning beees identify cells that are infested with varroa, uncap these cells and remove diseased brood.

Whereas it was once possible to keep bees and more or less allow them to self manage their development, colony pressures, including afflictions such as the varroa parasite, have led beekeepers towards greater vigilance and intervention in the hive. 'Leave-alone' beekeeping, although once commonly practiced, has been replaced in recent decades by a series of monitoring, treatment and re-queening cycles. As most beekeepers are increasingly aware that their bees could succumb to all manner of parasites and viruses, it's now expected that they will keep a close eye out for any unhealthy changes to their colonies. The responsible beekeeper, rather than enjoying the one-time merits of allowing bees to develop healthier colonies with minimal intervention, will tend colonies regularly in an attempt to protect their health. Increased management in beekeeping has become both a practical necessity and the cultural norm.

Although some beekeepers may be interested in bucking this trend and reducing hive management to increase honeybee and varroa co-adaptation, the conditions of most modern apiculture restrict rather than encourage non-intervention. Beekeepers who might consider allowing their colonies to swarm and adapt to the varroa mite through natural selection would probably have to recreate the circumstances and principles of the Gotland Bond Project to a degree that just isn't possible for the majority. While the experiment on Gotland was never intended as a model for beekeeping practice, it certainly highlights the difficulties beekeepers face. Whereas Gotland's isolation enabled an experiment at distance from standard external influences, most European beekeeping is practiced in more populous areas. Although many beekeepers maintain few colonies, the proximity of neighbouring apiaries adds to overall population density. Bees within apiaries at close quarters compete for forage, for example, as well as potentially transmit disease and mate with other subspecies. For beekeepers to approach non-intervention within the hive, they would need to consider the impact of other farming practices that occur beyond the hive and that of neighbouring beekeepers as well. For honeybee and varroa adaptation to be plausible, broad agreement of non-intervention would first be necessary, at least at a regional level.

The legislation of beekeeping can be controversial and difficult to enforce, as evidenced by the disagreement between supporters of native species beekeeping and subspecies importation in Læsø, another Scandinavian island off the coast of Denmark. In this case, the work of beekeepers nurturing the island's native black bee, *Apis mellifera mellifera*, who were supported by an EU ruling in 1993 to restrict the transportation of other subspecies to Læsø, was ultimately undermined by a small number of beekeepers who wanted to continue importing stock. One beekeeper in particular who argued his right to keep what he considered more productive, non-native bees, such as the Italian bee, *Apis mellifera ligustica*, fuelled the debate by refusing to comply with the ruling. After various court hearings, the European Court concluded that this beekeeper's actions were illegal and therefore maintained its order to develop Læsø as a honeybee conservation area. The victory was short lived: a change in national government brought a new Minister of Agriculture and Food who soon overturned this decision and reinstated honeybee trading in 2005. Unfortunately, even on a small island with few bees and people, it took the catalyst of a single beekeeper's disagreement with a policy encouraging local adaptation for free-trade to overwhelm the more long-term ideals of conservation. Encouragingly, as of January 2014, a concurrent ruling by the Scottish government supports native black bee conservation areas on the Hebridean islands of Colonsay and Oronsay where colonies are considered varroa-free. Although the black bees on these islands can't compensate for the species diversity that could have been encouraged on Læsø, this is a significant opportunity to develop the same subspecies renowned for its suitability to northern biomes.

Now that distinct European honeybee subspecies are rarities, the principles of good beekeeping have become all the more complex. In densely-populated areas such as England, where the regular importation of different subspecies has led to the hybridisation of most colonies, any beekeeper wanting to stock a particular import is caught in a recurring cycle of re-queening to avoid the very hybrids that this practice causes. Beekeepers on Læsø, meanwhile, who want to sustain subspecies distinction for the converse purpose of conserving a native bee, also need to check colonies for any sign of hybridisation. Queens that have interbred with imported stock are then removed. In other locations where beekeepers are already assured the benefits of a native and locally reared subspecies – as in Slovenia with the carniolan bee – queens that display the telltale markings of another subspecies are similarly picked out to keep colonies distinct. Whereas this intervention is considered necessary to maintain healthy colonies that are naturally adapted to their region, on Gotland non-intervention has allowed the honeybee to adapt naturally, in this case to a parasite. Even non-intervention can represent a form of management, however; by *placing* colonies in an isolated environment, scientists were able to monitor their ability to survive varroa through swarming. Although swarming is commonly perceived as a colony out of control, the Gotland Bond Project offers an insight into the potential for natural honeybee adaptation.

In our hands, the honeybee is a species that traverses and works a highly-populated and managed European landscape. Although honeybee management is without doubt necessary within such a demanding contemporary environment, perhaps developing more opportunities for this species to newly benefit from natural adaptation is overdue. While commercial breeding and transportation have curtailed the European honeybee's natural evolution, these case studies open discourse about the disadvantages of overt intervention and the merits of more considerate management. By minimising the global transportation of bees, encouraging the regional adaptation of subspecies through local queen rearing and only implementing non-invasive hive management techniques, we might progress healthier colonies and a more responsible and sustainable co-existence with the honeybee.

conservation

five

High above street level, safe in its seclusion, a fresh buzz in the air emanates from one of many new rooftop apiaries. From down below little is apparent, and yet up here within this discrete location it's clear that something special is occurring. Flowerpots brimming with colour, style and stamen provide a taster. Streams of worker bees, mesmerising in their composed flight, are repeatedly travelling to and from their hives in search of further urban forage. A rare, solitary carpenter bee – all the more conspicuous in amongst the many – sedately passes by. Having already seen honeybees thrive in the far north at remove from agriculture, it's intriguing to consider that areas more renowned for concrete than crops might also provide productive alternatives to apiculture's standard rural surroundings.

The recent transformation of urban off-spaces into apiaries is advantageous for beekeeper and bees. The honeybee, subjected to cold extremes in remote locations, is protected by warmer temperatures within the city's built environment. In contrast to foraging wild flower meadows and forests, city bees visit parks and gardens to feed from a broad range of decorative cultivars and specimen trees. As hives can be kept close at hand, city beekeepers benefit from ready access to colonies that they can check regularly and themselves receive support from various local organisations. With urban beekeeping on the rise, existing beekeeping associations have indeed become all the more active in responding to requests for advice from businesses, councils, community groups and individuals with budding apicultural aspirations.

Much of this new interest in beekeeping has been motivated by heightened awareness of recent honeybee decline. The oft-paraphrased prediction, which warns us that if bees disappear, we'll also perish, has intensified a sense of co-dependency with honeybees. The physical distance and rationale we generally adopt to separate ourselves from bees – based on our fear of being too close to multitudinous stinging insects – has relaxed in favour of keeping a closer eye on them.* Those couple of hives that were unassumingly placed at the bottom of many people's gardens or on the edges of farms have been re-established in the margins of contemporary city spaces where most of us now live.

Extreme colony losses that initially occurred in the countryside have led to a sequence of wide-ranging responses, many of which have been instigated in the city. In the mid-1990s, for example, French beekeepers who began rapidly losing colonies located near synthetically treated crops were struck by a conflict of interest with arable farmers. Their advantageous collaboration was in jeopardy. Despite needing bees for pollination, those with land, crops and subsidy quotas to maintain seemed bound to the perceived advantage of synthetic chemical use for pest control. Campaigning beekeepers therefore looked to those who might consider the long-term agricultural importance of pollinators over short-term crop yields. Their protests resulted in media interest and drew a significant level of support from environmental organisations and public research institutions. As a result, the debate regarding bee health and agriculture progressed and became firmly connected with additional concerns of economics and nature conservation: the beekeeper's pragmatic concerns had taken a theoretical turn. New questions about the value of honeybees and whether we could afford to endanger such a beneficial subspecies began to

*Recommendations for the positioning of hives in densely populated areas relates to hedges and fences that help control the height of honeybee flight paths to reduce contact with humans.

alter our perception of beekeeping both in the countryside and in the city.

Olivier Darné
Artist beekeeper, Parti Poétique, St. Denis, Paris, France

I peer at the models in front of me, towering over their diminutive scale, reviewing at a glance Paris' development over the centuries. I'm in the city to meet a group of artists who've variously installed beehives in urban spaces and, on my way, have dropped by the Muséum National d'Histoire Naturelle where I've happened upon the museum's city plans depicting population growth. The models in front of me aren't new; Paris, represented by small, individually painted blocks, has long since morphed from green to grey, the city having rapidly consumed the once fertile land that would have supported earlier inhabitants. The building I'm standing in, one piece among the many, raised above ground by wrought ironwork, covers earth that would have once been prized for cultivating rather than accumulating specimens.

On my way downstairs, I saunter past giraffe methodically lined up alongside elephants, hyenas and other taxidermy in the central atrium, finding their life size comforting. Discrete exhibition barriers around the animals reinforce the reality of natural history collections: here there are no glass vitrines or painted panoramas to soften the macabre effect of a room full of dead animals.

As I leave the museum, still absorbed in its representation, I'm drawn to the bellow of what I assume to be yet another incarnation of natural history. From the sound, I picture London's dinosaur animatronics but, as I trace this nostalgic growl, I'm confronted by the 'Dodo Manège', a fairground carousel slowly rotating on its rusty axel. As it shudders and turns, the carousel incrementally reveals a toddler balanced in the arms of a model panda and an older child perched precariously one place behind on an oversized dodo. It's high time to get back to the bees.

137

* * *

By taking the train from central Paris to St. Denis, I'm travelling through the blur of two places conjoined and yet distinct. St. Denis, once famous in its own right for the basilica where the kings and queens of France were buried, has since been both assimilated by Paris and segregated by La Périphérique. I'm in this particular neighbourhood to meet Olivier Darné and Emmanuelle Roule who live and work here alongside their honeybees. In 2004, together with a group of co-workers, Olivier and Emmanuelle established the cultural group Parti Poétique based on Olivier's art practice, which since 1996 has been focused on re-engaging urban communities with nature. In this quieter residential pocket of built-up St. Denis, it's possible to second-guess the Parti Poétique door by the clean lines suggestive of a creative space. When Olivier answers the door and invites me inside, another world opens up: a small interior courtyard reveals a chicken roosting in a rabbit hutch and an array of plants lining the way to the studio. The studio itself is a well-organised, purpose-built space that resembles a beekeeper's store with honey jars rather than paintings or sculptures kept in storage.

The honey produced by Parti Poétique – aptly titled and simply labelled *Miel Béton* (*Concrete Honey*) – is made solely by bees located in urban environments. Hives, such as the 50 on St. Denis' city hall roof, are harvested of a rich honey that reflects the bees' forage sites, their *zone de butinage*. *Miel Béton*, analysed over a three-year period to ascertain the range of plants pollinated in the city compared with the countryside, was found to contain nectar and pollen from an extraordinarily wide variety of sources. Arnold Gérard from the Evolution, Genome, Speciation Laboratory, otherwise known to Olivier as 'Mr Bee', studied hives in St. Denis and an agricultural area 80km outside Paris by taking samples every 10 days from April to October. He also monitored the weight of the hives daily via scales linked to a GPS system. Olivier says that Arnold recorded a staggering 250 distinct flower sources in St. Denis compared with only 65 in the farmed location over the course of the experiment. The superior, complex flavour of honey combining all these city sources would seem to provide a healthier range of nutrition for bees.[1]* Cities may be more renowned for haute couture than horticulture but urban parks and gardens are increasingly providing more forage variety for bees than common rural spaces, in spite of what little green space is available. Cultivation in the countryside tends to increasingly result in intense areas of select forage, especially as meadows, orchards, hedgerows and diversified farming continue to disappear. Additionally, with the stress of productivity in the countryside, the use of invasive chemicals is that much more critical than in urban environments.

Speaking with Olivier, it's clear he shares the view that managing land solely for high productivity and profitability is detrimental to healthy biodiversity. He describes our rural, agricultural landscapes as *natur morte*: environments where nature is dead in practical and philosophical terms due to our treatment of crops without overall care for long-term soil fertility. As Olivier remarks, "bees are a life indicator" and once they show signs of distress we shouldn't disassociate our responsibility for the management of their well-being and the cause of their deaths.

The political aims of Parti Poétique are categorically positioned within an urban ecological debate, however, and, as their name suggests, this group is also lyrically engaged with the subject of nature's importance to city communities. One of the group's prominent projects, for example, is *Banque du Miel* (*Honey Bank*), which conceptually communicates an imperative and yet playful sentiment with the slogan 'Time is Honey'. The impact of contemporary economics on ecosystems obviously hasn't passed this socio-politically engaged group by, as the bank is often positioned in areas neighbouring financial centres such as the Paris stock exchange. The *Banque du Miel* offers the alternative

---

* Of course, as airborne pollutants such as lead originating from traffic exhaust can affect pollen and nectar, pollution is also a concern for bee health.

investment of a 'bee saving account'. Each account, for a small fee, entitles its investor – which as of 2012 numbered 1,000 – to a percentage of the honey harvest from bees they've supported directly, rather than money from honey sales. In fact, *Miel Béton* is always traded as a taste of the city rather than as a moneymaking product and a high percentage of the honey produced in the *Banque du Miel* also remains with the colony that made it. In its construction, the bank is an imposing container made from robust, utilitarian shipment materials made specifically for city centre locations. It is, in essence, an elaborate beehive built just tall enough to comply with the ruling of urban beekeeping in Paris, which requires hives to be isolated by at least a 2m high surround, and just wide enough for visitors to enter and observe bees in physical if not psychological comfort. One of Olivier's initial interests in the project was to explore the fascination and fear we now have of nature. Our distance in cities from practical, everyday ecology has led to a general disassociation with nature and the *Banque du Miel* temporarily brings what is normally outdoors into the interior world of human understanding.

Another of Parti Poétique's projects aimed at creating a more permanent opportunity for people to re-engage with ecology is *Zone Sensible*, an open-access space for bees to be housed alongside people here in St. Denis. Olivier explains that *Zone Sensible* may be a building site at present but it will soon combine gardens and a rooftop apiary with an exhibition and events space for artists, botanists, town planners, anthropologists, walkers, beekeepers and local residents. We go and see how work is coming along. After strolling only a couple of short side streets from the studio, we meet collaborators Pierre Gardent and Sylvan Bonnet who are busy constructing value from a previously disused and uncared for corner of the city. Sure enough, *Zone Sensible*, which when carefully translated suggests a slum area made into a place for the senses, is totally transformed the next time I see it. The second time I meet and speak with Olivier, we can sit on deckchairs and drink in both the springtime sun and herbal tea made from *Zone Sensible* plants while its bees are off foraging the neighbourhood.

I ask Olivier what's new for Parti Poétique's conceptual and practical 'Pollination of the City' and he immediately tells me about *Banque de Reine* (*Queen Bank*), an initiative to rear queens for local hives. Using a process of artificial swarming, the group is increasing the amount of queens and fledgling colonies by 100 a year in a project that was set up as a prototype in 2011 and launched in 2014. The concept of saving bees by investing in the bank project has clearly developed into insurance against colony losses too. For the group to now be producing replacement queens as a priority, the importance of maintaining strong colony numbers has obviously become even more significant than honey production. Whereas honey is symbolic of a wealth of natural produce, queens and their colonies are indicative of the health of natural environments. Additionally, the importance of rearing healthy bees to the best of our abilities for pollination suggests a useful parallel to creating supportive environments in which to propagate ideas within urban communities about the connectivity of nature.

By bringing art and apiculture together within an urban environment, Parti Poétique is able to re-engage audiences with nature through direct experience. Like many city dwellers, Olivier has no background in farming – in fact, he learnt the first steps of beekeeping from an old book, he says – and therefore encountered a steep learning curve when starting out. It may be in spite or because of this that Parti Poétique projects are always so energetically undertaken with education in mind. As we take a closer look at the 25 hives on the *Zone Sensible* roof, it's reassuring to think that the kids playing nearby on Astro Turf know about their local bees from the weekly workshops that take place here. Indeed, as the bees fly purposefully past our heads, there's no need for any apprehension whatsoever; the spectacle of nature in the city that Parti Poétique explored in earlier work has been resoundingly replaced by the integration of bees within this urban environment. Through stable, long-term support of the project, Parti Poétique's work in St. Denis is understood and appreciated as a fine opportunity to reconnect with ecology at a time when our engagement with nature critically needs bringing back to life.

The success of Parti Poétique's projects reflects an encouraging level of interest for nature within the city. An urban public already aware of severe colony losses in France and elsewhere has been presented opportunities to better engage with honeybees through the organisation's immersive approach. Whereas 'the environment' can be a distant, abstract concept, initiatives such as *Zone Sensible* in St. Denis provide the means to understand environmental concerns on a more local, direct and personal basis. Indeed, as the trend for more and more of us to move to the city continues, any hope of retaining some meaningful appreciation of ecosystems needs to be established closer to home. Our curiosity for information about the natural world may not have diminished but our hands-on engagement with flora and fauna has decreased to the point that many of us are reduced to experiencing nature through educational yet sterile natural *history*. Beekeeping provides an ideal means to practically re-engage with the plants and animals that are integral to ecosystems. Working with honeybees connects horticulture with husbandry and food production; it increases our responsibility for maintaining healthy, biodiverse environments.

A comparable project in London, which was instigated in line with the onset of UK colony losses, similarly focuses on developing greater re-engagement with nature through beekeeping in the city. The high profile 'Capital Bee Campaign' – funded by the Mayor's Office and organised by Sustain, the UK charity that produces research and projects regarding food and farming policy – established 50 new community apiaries across the city from 2010 to 2012. Under the umbrella of 'Capital Growth', which encourages communities to grow their own food in London, Sustain's aim was to add honey to the food being produced independently while simultaneously creating a pollinator base for those crops being grown. After consultation with a variety of community groups, seven experts were selected to provide education to budding beekeepers from schools, parks, allotments and businesses. The following year, new hives were built from UK-sourced cedar* and stocked with Buckfast bees from East Surrey. Advertising keyed into public awareness of honeybees in decline by depicting bee specimens in cartoon environments being animated back to health.† The project initially presented a breadth of promise. Unfortunately, in its first operational year the UK was blighted by particularly poor spring weather, making it too wet for bees to forage and conditions difficult for novice beekeepers to manage. As newly established Buckfast colonies started to swarm, feral bees, diminished colonies and virgin queens mating with other local drones would all have been just concerns. Handling fifty beekeeping sites throughout London is a more demanding proposition than fifty hives in one apiary on top of the city hall in St. Denis, especially with new beekeepers. The full ambition behind London's campaign, while admirable, was almost impossible to realise, therefore. Despite these pragmatic challenges, Mikey Tomkins who managed the Capital Bee Campaign from March 2011,

---

* Cedar is a popular wood for beehives for several reasons: as a softwood, it's lightweight; containing natural oils, it's less likely to warp – unlike pine, another popular softwood hive material – and doesn't need to be painted with chemical preservatives; it's rot-resistant; and tends not to get infested by bugs.

† Having used dead bees in combination with hand-drawn elements, the Capital Bee Campaign's advertising is more stark than animation that utilises the Disney-effect to engage audiences but is nevertheless equally anthropomorphic.

remains genuinely optimistic about the value of having created spaces in the city that have since become centres of ecological knowledge. In conversation, Mikey explains that the project's aim was to expand urban appreciation of the connections between nature and farming, focusing attention away from mass production towards the interconnectivity of ecosystems, food production and consumption.

In the wake of honeybee decline, a number of campaigns, initiatives and projects have been established in the UK of which 'Plan Bee', the Co-operative Group's bid as a high street food retailer to improve pollinator health and habitat, remains the largest. When discussing the publication of *A World Without Bees*, Alison Benjamin relates her satisfaction with the influence her book had on the Co-op director's decision to withdraw neonicotinoids from the company's fruit and vegetable production in 2009, significantly ahead of the EU suspension. Plan Bee has since developed into a breadth of funded initiatives ranging from a community meadow project to urban beekeeping support. The Co-op also financed the production of *Vanishing of the Bees*, a 2009 documentary highlighting the plight of honeybees.

Smaller yet similarly funded private sector projects are exampled by design company Wolff Olins' 'Honey Club' in King's Cross, North London. As a collaborative project with the charity Global Generation, the Honey Club has developed honey production from a couple of hives located on the company's rooftop garden into an innovative social enterprise. Local businesses and institutions that invest £2,000 a year in the club support beekeeping, an educational programme for local secondary school pupils, and fund the organisation of annual workshops about bees, pollination and honey-related topics. Within its second operational year, the club's honey was already available for sale and there were plans to extend the project to another location in Angel, Islington.

All in all, through the initiatives of individuals, communities and businesses, beekeeping in London more than doubled over a four-year period. Official figures for Greater London from 'BeeBase', the National Bee Unit within the Food & Environment Research Agency (FERA), registered 1,617 colonies in 2008 and 3,337 in 2012.[2] Of course, this rapid increase in the number of colonies has intensified London's hive density. Angela Woods, secretary of the London Beekeepers Association (LBKA) from 2011 to 2014, supposes that 2,000 hives exist within a 10km radius of her inner city apiary. Her figures are corroborated in Mikey Tomkin's detailed and considered study of urban beekeeping in *Second Nature Urban Agriculture* (2014), which states:

> ... within a 3km radius [the mean used to measure standard distances covered by worker bees] of central London (Trafalgar Square) there are 150 colonies (50 apiaries) at a density of one hive per 19ha. By comparison, as we start to move out to 20km from the centre there are 3,999 colonies (1,333 apiaries) with a much lower density of one hive per 31ha.[3]

In combination, Mikey and Angela's statistics suggest the more central the London location, the more densely-populated with honeybee colonies it will have become.

Although neither of the two would want to discourage any new beekeeper, their figures raise concerns about the management of so many colonies. From distinct perspectives, Mikey considers that sustainable beekeeping could come from shared knowledge within urban communities, while Angela thinks beekeeping should be monitored to encourage responsible care. She describes the 20 swarms retrieved from the same location near her home in 2012 which she suggests points to the same beekeeper or beekeepers repeatedly losing primary swarms from a nearby apiary. Although much advice exists and beekeeping is often undertaken seriously and studiously, current legislation allows practitioners to keep bees without registration and therefore some beekeepers fall outside systems of monitoring and guidance.[4]* Some beekeepers, for example, now follow the most up-to-date advice on stocking hives with locally reared bees, but the trend of importing bees from further afield still prevails.[5]† FERA's advice on imported colonies includes detail of EU legislation for the transportation of bees that largely refers to the prevention of disease transmission.‡ It makes no mention of local adaptation and therefore inadvertently supports the ongoing global transportation of *Apis mellifera* subspecies, in keeping with our taste for exotic honey. Bees reared in New Zealand that produce Manuka honey, for example, also make popular honeybee queen exports for the UK market.[6]§ While London does not as yet have a queen-rearing programme, a system such as Parti Poétique's in St. Denis could be a means to

---

* The LBKA estimate a further 25% unregistered colonies exist in London.

† In 2013, 8,625 queens were imported from other EU Member States into the UK, the top three export countries being Greece (4,393 queens), Italy (1,330 queens) and Slovenia (1,140 queens). One likely cause for this high number of imports points to significant colony losses from the winter of 2012–13. The previous year, a similarly high number of queen were imported, however: a total 7,977 queens with the top three importers being Greece (3,650), Slovenia (1,567) and Denmark (1,066). In 2007, the first year of the Beebase record, 7,741 queens were imported, predominantly from Greece (5,129), Cyprus (1,146) and Slovenia (1,074).

‡ The EU directive known as the 'Balai Directive' (92/65/EEC) requires an original health certificate valid for 10 days that confirms bees are free from American Foul Brood, Small Hive Beetle and any Tropilaelaps mites before they're traded within EU Member States. The Commission Decision (2003/881/EC) assigns further regulations for exports from 'Third Countries' outside the EU.

§ In 2013, 520 queens were transported from New Zealand to the UK, a marked reduction from the 1,050 queens imported in 2010 but still a number that is surprising considering EU advice to reduce 'Third Country' imports.

develop the city's local honeybee gene pool in order to maintain better control of colony behavioural traits.

An even larger concern regarding honeybee population density in London is insufficient forage. To explain the extent of the problem, Angela presents a domestic analogy, suggesting that we wouldn't bring more and more cats into our home without giving them more food. More bees require more forage and a doubling of colonies raises the concern that competition for inner city forage is too high. In 2012, when an extremely cold and wet UK spring and summer critically reduced the honeybee's ability to source less profuse forage, beekeepers from north to south recorded colonies with limited honey stores.[7] Poor honey harvests averaging only 3.6kg (8lbs) throughout the UK were all the more impoverished in London, however, where an average 2.5kg (5.6lbs) per colony was recorded.[8]* As the bees we keep today in northern Europe tend to produce colonies that need at least 16–18kg (35–40lbs) of honey to overwinter alone, it's hard to imagine enough forage ever being achievable for the number of colonies in the capital. In 2013, London's average honey harvest improved but at 7.2kg (19lbs) was still significantly below the required minimum to assist colony stability. Concerns of limited forage are shared by Alison Benjamin and Brian McCallum:

> If we are serious about halting the decline of honeybees, we can't blithely introduce thousands more colonies into urban areas without being aware of the potential consequences if there is scant forage to sustain them.[9]

---

*The British Beekeepers Association annual honey survey of 2012 reported a 78% reduction in honey harvests in Greater London and a 72% reduction across the entire UK when compared with 2011 figures based on an annual average of 13.6kg (30lbs).

Although London is renowned for its wealth of parks and gardens, a 2010 study assessing changing approaches to garden planning in the city from 1998 to 2008 – produced by Chloë Smith on behalf of the London Wildlife Trust, Greenspace for Greater London and the Greater London Authority – identifies a significant reduction in wildlife habitat.[10] Analysis of aerial photographs from this period show the upward trend to home owners to install hard surfacing over green space, for example, and reinforce the need for public programmes such as 'Wild London'.[11] A parallel study, undertaken from 2010 to 2011 by Mihail Garbuzov at the Laboratory of Apiculture and Social Insects (LASI), University of Sussex, scientifically determines the varieties of garden plants that honeybees and other pollinators forage.[12] The gardener's observation that bees visit some flowers more than others is now supported by evidence which concurs that not all flowers are equally attractive to honeybees. From 32 varieties of flowering garden plants that were tested at the LASI research garden, it was discovered that borage – the fine blue flower renowned for its medicinal qualities – was their favourite. In contrast, workers showed little interest in highly-popular garden plant varieties of *Pelargonium*, commonly known as geraniums.* In combination, these studies suggest that London's green spaces can only help support London's growing number of colonies if reconsidered for pollinators. As encouragement to those Londoners who would like to be involved, the LBKA has produced a seed mix for year-round flowering plants that are attractive to pollinators, providing a handy means to engage with bees without becoming a beekeeper. The established

* It is considered that honeybees are not attracted to red flowers because they are unable to see the wavelength of light reflected by the colour. They also find little nutritional value in other visually exuberant blooms commonly appealing to gardeners, such as double-headed chrysanthemums, that aren't easily accessible to most pollinators because their pollen and nectar is overtly obscured.

profile of the association enables it to support beekeeping and its members by focusing current debate on increasing food for existing honeybee colonies in London. By operating as an intermediary between businesses, councils and the public, the LBKA aims to encourage a restorative balance between colony numbers and amounts of forage.

Caroline Birchall
Small-scale beekeeper, ecologist and Bee Collective founder
London, UK

In my final stride from A to B, the rumble of London Victoria's hustle and bustle, its stations and shopping, thoroughfare and interchange, all dissipate. Although I've never been to this particular spot before, I recognise this part of the city well. Its narrow way, ornate function and warehouse-to-residential conversions present a familiar backdrop and there's nothing more than the occasional black cab or passer-by with luggage to slow down my stompingly early arrival until the railings I find at the address in my notes. Though barring my entrance, they allow a view of whitewashed walls decorated with the outline of cartoon bees, adding curves to the angular. I'm obviously in the right place, so I wait by the gate.

When Caroline Birchall arrives with Paul Anthony Campbell a few minutes later, to their surprise and mine, I'm already inside. A split second decision to accept the offer of someone leaving the building has left me behind bars. From what I've heard about Caroline, we share the same interest and so it's a pleasure to be invited into the building beyond the courtyard in order to discuss ecology from her side of the fence.

Caroline, who's the founder of the Bee Collective, and Paul, the organisation's strategic advisor, immediately huddle a few chairs together in the centre of the room. This practical rather than snug space, pulling the warm air from our breath on this sharp winter's day, would provide just the right conditions for harvesting honey in the summer; the Bee Collective, which launched in 2012, offers a honey extraction service for London beekeepers. I can easily imagine this room brimming with activity, the indomitably sweet and musky fragrance of honey and wax permeating the room. The clear organisation of such a neat space would be pleasantly disrupted when the wax seals from frames are sliced back to reveal the golden harvest. The only evident equipment, a stainless steel centrifuge, would then turn the open frames to draw honey from the comb into multiple glass jars beneath. Honey extraction, like other beekeeping activities, is very hands-on and indeed time-consuming. As this sticky business can be difficult for beekeepers to perform at home, the Bee Collective provides dedicated space and tools for the job. The project was initiated with financial backing and funding in-kind from the private sector through the Victoria Business Improvement District in order to support otherwise independent beekeepers and, as a result, necessarily follows a business model itself. Each beekeeper that uses the Bee Collective's service receives a high-quality, unblended product in return for 10% of their harvest plus the cost of materials paid in either cash or honey. The year's honey collection is then sold and the proceeds contribute towards raising funds and awareness for urban forage development. Although a couple of hives return little honey, especially given current conditions in London, the value of an extraction service lies in collectivising beekeeping practices rather than producing vast profit. With more and more beekeepers in London, there's increasing need for facilities and organisations that group small-scale operations together. This business provides both a practical service, therefore, and a means to exchange urban beekeeping knowledge and experiences.

Importantly, for this practice to be a success the Bee Collective is extending its scope beyond these four walls. Although only in its formative stages, the initiative is being expanded to include as many collaborative ventures as possible such as its work with the LBKA and Urban Bees. During our enthused conversation, further warmed with generous mugs of good, strong tea, Caroline discusses a wide breadth of other possible opportunities including the use of excess wax to make candles by a local organisation for people with learning difficulties, a venture with Neal's Yard Remedies, and another with the Golden Company to produce cosmetics. Through varied collaborations, the Bee Collective aims to maximise all the potential uses of its produce, creating rich networks in the process.

As an ecologist who used to work as a bee scientist at Rothamsted agricultural research centre in Hertfordshire, Caroline's other major means of supporting the honeybee is through her work as an advisor for Natural England, the governmental body that counsels on the environment. Caroline's keen interest in placing beekeeping and pollination within an environmental context is currently focused on a major project advancing pollinator habitat. In collaboration with Buglife, the UK charity dedicated to sustaining levels of insect, spider and worm populations, Natural England plans to connect and extend existing pollinator habitat across the whole country. With the financial support of the Co-operative Group, 'B-Lines' has been launched with a pilot project in Yorkshire known as 'Bee-Roads'.* The plan is to utilise sites of importance for nature conservation – known in shorthand as 'sinc' – as core habitat and to connect them with stepping stone spaces within the B-Lines project. In London, for example, existing pollinator habitat such as the Lea Valley and the grasslands of South London could be joined together by two or three wild flower B-Lines. Rather than London B-Lines then ending at the ring road of the M25, the intention would be to link them with farmland beyond the city's limits. A new map of England,

---

* The pilot project has been named to accommodate reference to both the Co-op's project, Plan Bee, and that of Natural England.

plotting expansive, interconnected pollinator habitat, is certainly a satisfying proposition.

In line with a key Natural England remit, B-Lines aims to restore insect biodiversity throughout England. As Caroline explains, the UK government's biodiversity strategy – previously based on a series of white papers assessing national ecosystems that focused on improving habitat for monitored species within set locations – has been redefined in an attempt to redress an ongoing decline in biodiversity. In order to succeed where other projects have failed, B-line organisers now consider that they need to encourage landowners, managers and officials to recognise the benefits of pollinators and their habitats. The government's renewed methodology is aimed at both public and private sectors developing a landscape-scale approach to habitat conservation and species biodiversity which would bring town and city planning together with agricultural, manufacturing and leisure industries within a connected land management strategy. In keeping with Natural England's new phrasing of ecology, Caroline describes pollinator habitat as 'a functioning landscape' to convey the use-value of land that might not otherwise exist with so many different interests involved. Through our discussion, I'm beginning to appreciate just how delicate the balance being struck between the private sector, public bodies and environmental advisors currently is.

Within Caroline and Paul's work at the Bee Collective, honey is the classic means being used to represent a process that would otherwise be difficult to quantify. In using it to promote pollinator habitat and forage, however, honey becomes an ecological product with a worth more precious than its already nutritional value and sweetness. When in short supply, as is currently the case in London, Bee Collective honey might become all the more exclusive, so when Caroline passes me a small jar of honey, just as Olivier Darné had done in St. Denis, I appreciate her gesture. Although operational within a commercial context, Paul reflects that the focus of the Bee Collective is "less about money and more about the message" and for Caroline, who wants to communicate a positive message that "isn't all doom and gloom", the hope is to increase awareness and business collaborations that will impact a new phase of decisions and action to conserve those all important bees sooner rather than later.

⁓

In attempting to reframe nature's worth for those whose commercial activities otherwise reduce natural habitat and species diversity, environment advisors, campaigners and researchers have adopted the language of business and economics. For ecologists like Caroline, applying terminology such as 'ecosystem services' with reference to 'natural capital'* is intended to provide owners, managers and users of land with a quantifiable role for nature within their businesses. As honey currently has low market value, crop yields are increasingly used as a tangible end product to commercially verify pollinator habitat:

> Through enhancing the yield of many high value
> crops, pollination is worth between £430m and
> £510m to the UK economy.[13]

In this instance, figures suggest that without considering pollinators both growers and suppliers risk reduced harvests and profits. Although bees and other pollinators collectively forage a diverse range of wild and cultivated flowering plants, this now common perception positions pollinators and their worth only in relation to our crop harvests. Another important example, based on research undertaken at Reading University and included in the Friends of the Earth 'Bee Cause' campaign,

* Coined by US conservationist, Mark Tercek, onetime managing director of Goldman Sachs, now president and CEO of Nature Conservancy.

calculates the cost of replacing insect pollination with hand pollination in the UK at £1.8 billion a year.[14] The projected cost of such work, in this case, places a value on the otherwise free work of pollinators. Natural capital calculations in the UK suggest that agriculture would be exorbitantly expensive to sustain without pollinators.

By identifying the economic value of nature, we may have found a means to challenge current policies that otherwise overlook ecology, but what might be the ultimate price if nature's cultural worth becomes predominantly monetary, especially in economically unstable times? As with all commercial activity, the business potential of nature is likely to affect risks as well as rewards. In describing the natural world predominantly in terms of business, we give nature a role to perform and place ourselves in a managerial position of authority. As conservationist Tom Butler emphatically states:

> Even as humanity lives by the grace of nature, our language generally conveys a relationship of ownership. We speak of protecting 'our' oceans or forests. Areas that we exploit for economic gain are 'working landscapes'. The living Earth becomes 'natural resources' to be developed or 'natural capital' to be valued. These metaphors perpetuate the delusion that our species isn't a member in the community of life but a global technocrat managing commodities.[15]

Categorising pollinator habitat as a 'working landscape' may allow it to compete with the use-value of agricultural land but in effect turns habitat into a commodity. By the same measure, pollinating insects also become commodities when we describe part of their feeding cycle as an 'ecosystem service'. Indeed, we're steadily developing a perception of pollinators as 'pollination service providers'. While we already regard the honeybee as our honey producer, by increasingly focusing on *Apis mellifera* as a key pollinator of crops, we additionally perceive the bee as our pollination worker. Although commercial operations already exist where beekeepers agree the annual cost of pollination services with arable farmers, the danger of putting an overall price on pollination could be that pollinators are then considered replaceable, at the right price. By focusing on the economic short-term gains of the honeybee as a 'service provider', we risk undervaluing the inherent long-term of nature and dismissing the more cautionary significance of the honeybee as a 'life indicator'.

In contrast to natural capital, concern regarding honeybee decline has also been much more emotively expressed. In 2009, when UK beekeepers first marched on Downing Street, London, and petitioned the government to increase research funding in order to 'save our bees',[16] their protest was an independent call for support after their excessive personal losses. Investigative journalism generated interest that in turn generated more copy about a wide range of honeybee and beekeeping related stories, including material that soon progressed to include advice on how to help *conserve* bees. The death of honeybees which started as the beekeeper's personal loss has within a short time developed into a public loss that suggests our collective responsibility for the insect.

While we seem generally keen on eradicating insects, the unusual call to save one species in particular has additionally led to further consideration of wild pollinator conservation. As scientific research has incrementally come to fruition, questions that were originally raised in relation to the honeybee have subsequently been asked about other pollinators. In particular, the European Commission's report based on the EFSA's Pesticide Peer Review (2013) has been instrumental in highlighting a lack of studies determining the effects of synthetic agricultural chemicals on other insects. Studies specifically focused on wild insects, meanwhile, have substantiated concerns that species are being lost at an exponential rate.[17] As a consequence, media comment now commonly incorporates all bee pollinators in one:

> ... half the UK's honeybees kept in managed hives have gone, wild honeybees are close to extinction and solitary bees are declining in more than half the places they have been studied.[18]

In this instance, in order to highlight the magnitude of pollinator losses, a distinction has been made between kept and wild honeybees – although they are the same species – with added reference to solitary bees. The wild and domestic traits of the European honeybee that already complicate its description are being compounded by this association with wild pollinators. As a result, contemporary campaigning that aims to raise public awareness and support pollinator health often blurs bee references, as exampled by Bee Cause publicity, which with the slogan 'sow your seeds, save the bees' states:

> Britain's bees are in trouble. Their habitat is vanishing. Their numbers are falling fast. And that leaves us in big trouble too, since we need these busy little creatures to pollinate our fruit and vegetable crops. So please text ... to get your bee-friendly wild flower seeds and grow a garden that'll help bees – and the rest of us – to thrive.[19]

Within just a few lines, this worthy charitable cause merges a breadth of factors, referring to both wild bees and honeybees without clear distinction. When we read that "bees are in trouble", we may recall the demise of honeybees near sunflower fields, and yet any reference to "habitat" partially discounts those very same colonies. Unlike wild bees, kept bees – which account for the vast majority of European honeybees – are hived creatures that require habitat only as forage. Within large colonies, honeybees feed from a broad range of plants in contrast to the selective habits of wild solitary bees. Although "our fruit and vegetable crops" can be pollinated by a range of insects, the reality of our predominantly monoculture crops is that they require dedicated, intensive pollination: namely by the honeybee. While concern for wild pollinators is critical and a garden grown with bee-friendly wild flower seeds beneficial, conflating references to kept and wild bees encourages the impression that to 'save *the* bees' it's sufficient to employ small-scale, independent conservation measures.

Other equally well-meaning attempts to help conserve the honeybee have confused the overall needs of bees as quantitative rather than qualitative, leading to many more people taking up beekeeping. Angela Woods challenges this approach by comparing it with other forms of animal conservation, suggesting that we wouldn't go out, buy and keep a wild cat – a White Tiger, for instance – if we wanted to save the species. By evoking a wild animal rather than a pet and flipping her previous domestic cat analogy, she clearly states that we've misread the needs of honeybees. As a managed creature under our care, the honeybee is obviously different to the Giant Panda, and although it's now within the realm of wildlife conservation to care for animals in captivity, it's still unusual to consider the conservation of a creature kept for its productivity. When BSE threatened the lives of many cattle in 1984, although highly distressing, there was no outcry to save cows. Similarly when outbreaks of Foot and Mouth Disease occurred in 2001 and 2007, cows, pigs and sheep were culled and then replaced. So what indeed does it mean to call for the conservation of a farmed creature?

Our 'life indicator' honeybee is suffering from all manner of stresses, which raise pertinent questions of our stewardship and signify the increasingly impoverished state of agricultural environments. As these are highly-managed landscapes, just as the honeybee is a highly-managed insect, it should be within our capability to take better care of farming practices. Through our lack of direct involvement in food production, we appear to have relinquished interest in the richness of our primary culture, agriculture. With new public concern for the honeybee and engagement with beekeeping, however, we could connect the value of growing bee-friendly flowers in city gardens with the need to produce bee-friendly crops in the countryside as well.[20]* While there are certainly physical distances between urban and rural spaces that often lead to disassociation, our dependency on the countryside for food and energy supplies shouldn't be underestimated; it's within the best interest of urban populations to reconnect with rural land use and farming practices. Fortunately, we're already fascinated with a practice that enables us to do just that.

When Angela Woods discusses the LBKA's current strategy of increasing forage rather than beekeepers in London, she suggests on reflection that "we are all beekeepers whether we keep bees or not" and in return it seems appropriate to ask whether as a practicing urban beekeeper she considers herself a farmer. Without any pause for thought, Angela says "yes" and then after only a brief moment's consideration adds with conviction, "I'm a small-scale urban farmer." She goes on to describe beekeeping

---

* In fact, a LASI study undertaken from August 2009 to July 2011, published in 2014, identifies the higher-level value of rural areas compared with urban areas for pollinators when managed under 'Agri-Environment Schemes' (AES) intended to increase plant biodiversity.

as a form of meditation that she nevertheless appreciates is also husbandry. "I don't romanticise my bees", she says, "6,000 stinging insects are my responsibility." Alison Benjamin's thoughts on the same question return a manifold answer: while her partner and collaborator, Brian McCallum, considers their bees as livestock, Alison wonders whether something might be lost in our relationship with the honeybee if we simply describe beekeeping as farming. As Brian regularly tends their bees and demonstrates honeybee husbandry for educational purposes, Alison suggests that out of the two of them he takes the more pragmatic approach to their projects. Caroline Birchall on the other hand, after some contemplation, proposes that her potential role as a farmer is more dependent on pollination than husbandry: only if her colony pollinated crops such as apple trees would Caroline consider herself a farmer. Additionally, as Caroline's bees only produce small quantities of honey, she considers her harvest or 'farmed produce' to be minimal. "I'm a beekeeper for the bees", she says, describing her beekeeping practice as the diligent care of a living organism. Mikey Tomkins, meanwhile, having freshly written an article about urban agriculture and beekeeping, seems a likely candidate to describe himself as an urban farmer and yet surprisingly says, "actually, no, I don't live in London!" His is the somewhat rare and necessary voice of someone living in the countryside who campaigns for farming's relevance in the city. He quotes Camilla Goddard, the only commercial beekeeper that he's aware of in London, who says, "I see myself as an undercover farmer because my bees feed on everyone's land."

Encouragingly, we appear to be in a moment of transition where an individual's engagement with apiculture, and as a result agriculture, need not be distant and abstract but present, real and vital. If we're to seriously improve honeybee health and with it our own wellbeing, we need to make the most of this timely opportunity to realise a more interconnected approach to agriculture and ecology. We need fully support 'farming for the landless', for the honeybee, the beekeeper and the non-farming landless community we have largely become.

epilogue

Sylejman and Anyi Zogiani

Commercial beekeepers, Fushë Kosovë, Kosovo

The bountiful and dark fruit appears unbelievably ripe. Such a ready yet unfamiliar crop, hanging temptingly at a short picking distance away, is intriguing. Although nearby collections of cultivated plants – from golden chrysanthemums to sweet peas in pastel shades – form a more ornate spectacle, my focus remains fixed on that broad, gnarled tree in the centre of this secluded walled garden. Fruit-spoiled paving stones suggest that any purple, bauble-like berries falling into my hands won't be missed, and yet I instinctively look round all the same for any sign of witness. Only the most inconspicuous of visitors to the nearby flowers are out and about, however: abundant honeybee colonies are making the most of their immediate environment at this sacred Orthodox patriarchate near Pejë. I imagine previous worker bees pollinating the blossom on this tree earlier in the year and contemplate their mutually beneficial position within this protected enclosure.

When I sample a berry, it stains my fingertips and possesses a sugary sharpness that lingers on my tongue beyond its brief flavour. Only later will I truly appreciate the full bittersweet significance in tasting rather than wasting fruit from this very particular tree, the only mulberry I'll see in Kosovo. This is a country still reeling and recovering from the war in 1998–9 and nature remains a marked casualty. Trees, seen as an important resource previously withheld from Albanians, have been felled for firewood, both out of post-war necessity to keep warm before houses could be rebuilt and symbolically to claim land previously managed first by the Communist state and then by Serbian landowners. Although once common throughout this territory, mature fruit trees, including mulberry, apple, plum and quince, are now scarce within an open landscape surrounded by a mountain keep also being incrementally depleted of its forests. Kosovo, as a result, is woefully empty of the vegetation, cropping potential and cultural value its trees once provided. The berry I'm tasting, within the high walls of this UNESCO world heritage site patrolled by UN soldiers, has been coincidentally conserved inside one of few surviving local areas of mature cultivation.

Imported varieties of fruit such as the large American plum line shelves in newly opened supermarkets – with their modern approximations of edenic abundance and infinite provision – in place of the astoundingly rich, local crops that once abounded on market stalls. Although Kosovo benefits from a variety of microhabitats with diverse soil and climate influenced by the country's varied elevation from the plains to the mountains and its proximity to the Adriatic and the Aegean, very few crops are now grown here. A population, at one time almost two-thirds employed within the agricultural sector and yet significantly unwaged, in regrouping post-war, has on the whole decided not to farm;[1] returning and resident Kosovans increasingly live in the city. The earlier exchange of goods between farmers and the distribution of food from co-operative groups on behalf of the state has been replaced by a more familiar culture of consuming. Where money was once relatively redundant, expensive price tags are now common for products from large-scale operators in Bulgaria and Hungary and fresh produce from neighbouring Serbia and Macedonia. Kosovans, in common with most Europeans, are now reliant on imported food and increasingly face questions of economic and environmental suitability and sustainability.

* * *

I'm en-route to meet two Kosovan beekeeping elders on the new road between Prishtina and Pejë, which, although incomplete, is officially open and heaving with traffic. A heady concoction of dust, exhaust fumes and fresh asphalt permeates the midday heat. From my sweatbox, the majority of summer holiday traffic – mostly comprising of visiting emigrant families in brand new, air-conditioned Volkswagens and BMWs – looks calm, collected and conspicuous. The road we're sharing slices through desolate scenery. Our view is one devoid of focal points. The standard pinnacles of old buildings are all missing and there are no livestock or crops in sight. Beyond the road, we're surrounded by what appears to be a barren land.

Taking one of several small side roads into the countryside thankfully returns some humanity to this landscape and I soon reach my destination. The beekeepers' village is a welcome island within open terrain, its houses built at ad hoc angles to one another. From the edge of this apparent labyrinth, I wonder whether or not I'll recognise the beekeepers' homes. In rounding a corner, I immediately encounter row upon row of active beehives, however, and realise they'll be no problem: around 80 colonies are being kept centrally in the village alongside two houses in particular. Although I'm already accustomed to seeing beehives in all kinds of locations, I've never seen so many on someone's doorstep before. This is no small apiary at the bottom of the garden and it's dramatic to see so many hives located within a domestic environment. I speculate that the people in this neighbourhood must have absolutely no fear of bees to have accepted so many colonies living and working at such close quarters.

An apiary this size requires significant maintenance and is tended in partnership by brothers Sylejman and Ayni Zogiani. Like many other beekeepers, the Zogianis manage their colonies as a second occupation; both are maths teachers who found they were unable to earn sufficient income from education alone.

After deciding to develop their father's apiary, they soon expanded colony numbers and have since established another apiary near Ayni's wife's family home. In both places, the brothers have progressed their apicultural business without landownership; beekeeping as landless farming is proving a valuable prospect in an area with otherwise little emphasis on agriculture. As respected practitioners, they also contribute to an association of beekeepers who necessarily overcome nationalist and religious divisions to communicate between distinct communities in Kosovo, Serbia, Macedonia, Montenegro and Bulgaria.

I'm met by Ayni Zogiani who promptly proposes to celebrate my arrival with a honey tasting. From the sheltered area outside his modest, single-storey house, Ayni first introduces me to his wife and father. We then take our seats alongside a couple of nursery apple trees to sample the produce harvested from this very garden. To my surprise, the honey has a very distinctive and satisfyingly complex flavour. In fact, I decide it's the best honey I've ever tasted. Overlooking the hives, gardens and surroundings, while exploring this area by taste, it suddenly becomes possible to reconsider the landscape. I now realise, from this stationary perspective, that the barren land of my journey is full of flowers. Despite few crops and trees to forage, it's evident that honeybees can still flourish where wild flowers and herbaceous plants are spontaneously profuse. Could this landscape, at least for the bees, paradoxically be a richer environment through its lack of cultivation?

With matched enthusiasm, Ayni decides to show me the colonies that produce such extraordinarily good honey. As a precaution, I'm handed a mask reminiscent of the one I was given for my very first colony inspection with Edwin Clark in the UK. Ayni and his son then open up their only hive that's made from a sectioned, hollow tree trunk. Inside, an expansive honeycomb pattern fills every last gap, suggestive of productive, healthy bees with ample forage. The colony has extended the depth of their comb wherever possible, creating hexagonal cells with such depth that, in cross section on the lid of the hive, they resemble the fronds of bracken or fern. In being given a cylindrical rather than square container, these honeybees show the immediacy with which colonies will elaborate their already organic constructions. As an experiment rather than a museum piece, the tree trunk has been fitted with bespoke frames to enable a degree of routine hive management. Although, in trialling square pegs inside a round hole, the beekeepers may have compromised this nest's authenticity, their use of wood in its original form is more importantly emblematic of natural materials being kept from the fire.

Considering the breadth of their engagement, it's surprising to be told that both Sylejman and Ayni consider their apiary and beekeeping practice primitive. Despite their tree trunk hive being but a curio alongside many standard hives, these beekeepers seem to consider their entire operation old-fashioned. I tell them that their apicultural skill and intention is as incisive as the other expert beekeepers I've met and any sense of their operation being behind the times is unjustified. The centrifuge they use, for example, is the most sophisticated their machinery needs to be and is no different to any I've seen throughout Europe. As a principally manual practice on the periphery of agricultural intensification, beekeeping has remained largely unmechanised. Beekeepers still maintain their apiaries colony by colony to develop their efficiency and productivity. It's telling that the desire for these beekeepers to have the conveniences of modern life, once restricted and now ill-afforded, seem to outweigh an acute sense of how much they've actually achieved by hand.

When Sylejman invites me into his newly-constructed home, he tells me with justifiable satisfaction while gesturing around the lavish front room that "this house was built on honey". Like many other Kosovans, the Zogiani brothers are restructuring their homes post-war and yet, in contrast to the majority, have chosen to build on existing foundations. Due to a set of quite extraordinary circumstances, the Zogianis managed to stay in their village when war broke out. The family's otherwise perilous proximity to a major Serbian airbase kept the village intact, because it was considered less likely that NATO would bomb the base should civilians be living in the area; local families found a curious amnesty in homes located within one of Kosovo's most war-torn areas. As war raged on and food grew scarce, however, many left the area. For the brothers, their families and the 32 other people who eventually sought refuge nearby, when all other supplies had run dry, they still had a valuable store of honey. Without their apiary, the brothers know they couldn't have sustained themselves and their community, a memory that no doubt also resonates with their neighbours.

Many of those who were evacuated during the war are now returning and also rebuilding. As the UN's liberation strategies only extended into certain post-war development and systematic planning was slow to appear, many have been energetically developing land independently. After ten years of subservience under Milosevic's post-Yugoslav Serbia and even longer under the Communist state before that, a sudden lack of continuum in legislation allowed returning and resident populations to establish homes wherever and with whatever they could afford. New properties throughout Kosovo are, as a result, primarily large houses with substantial areas of enclosed land, separated by neat fencing, reflective of a post-Communist ideal.[2]* What was once farmland has been re-appropriated, regardless of its previous value, use and fertility. With so much construction liberally spread throughout Kosovo, the options for land-dependent farming practices are increasingly slight.

---

* Reports suggest that 15,000 houses were unofficially constructed to replace those destroyed during 1999 in the two to three year post-war period before the Ministry of Environment and Spatial Planning was established to implement strategies regulating municipal planning in Kosovo.

As landless farmers, Sylejman and Ayni Zogiani are currently benefiting from a landscape left fallow, and yet a landless country that relies solely on imports to feed its population would seem precarious. The immense jar of honey I collect from Sylejman and his eldest daughter in their small apicultural equipment store in Prishtina the next day far surpasses the quantity of usual city supplies. The equivalent honey in Paris and London, packaged and given in select amounts, is restricted in its quantity rather than quality by a heavily-populated built environment. Beyond these urban spaces, meanwhile, ever-distancing agriculture is burdened by increasing industrialisation affecting not only food quality but also its very ecology. As I leave the shop, I carry a generous jar of local produce wrapped modestly in newspaper that is plentiful, exceptional and yet full of portent.

—

Tiberiu and Mihaela Chirănescu
Migratory beekeepers, Dobruja, Romania

A close group of people, sheltering under the arbour of a few isolated trees, give and take a refreshing break from the surrounding monotony of yellow. While everything else withers on such a brilliantly bright day, sunflowers, with heads held uniformly high as far as the eye can see, collectively demonstrate the succinctness of their name. I'm on the road across Romania's flat east, south of the reedy Danube Delta. This area, once drained and reclaimed from the marshes, is now arid and yet still overwhelmingly agricultural. I'm scanning the landscape for markers and, on the next bend, I spot what appears to be a traditional caravan by the roadside. The closer I get, the more distinct the caravan continues to look until one side surprisingly reveals that it's full of beehives. A mobile home for both people and bees would be too interesting a discovery to miss.

Pulling off the road into a small clearing encourages a concealed dog to bark and a young boy to appear. Beside an oil drum stand of honey under the shade of a parasol, the boy attempts to demonstrate something that I've no hope of understanding with only a few basic phrasebook words. From the same nearby trees, a girl then arrives who, with the advantage of a couple more school years than her brother, manages to explain that the honey isn't for sale. As this surprising news doesn't lead to my anticipated departure, perplexed faces search mine until I manage to communicate with a series of gesticulations and smiles my interest in the hives. As a short message is obviously developing into a much longer conversation, the last two people resting under the trees decide to make their way towards the caravan. Before long, Tiberiu and Mihaela Chirănescu, who are now as intrigued as their children Razuan and Lavinia, also arrive to reunite the family once more.

I learn that the beekeepers are Seventh-Day Adventists and that I've arrived on their weekly day of rest. Not only is their honey therefore not for sale but Tiberiu and Mihaela are also fasting until sundown in respect of their faith. Although as a result I can only offer the children honey tea, I'm generously invited to stay for supper by their parents in return. As the afternoon is still young, the whole family is more than happy to show me around their mobile home-come-apiary in the meantime. Inside the caravan, a cosy living space – just about large enough to accommodate all of us while sitting – combines a cooking, living and sleeping area. The room appears to have been made with only one or two people in mind, so it's a challenge to imagine how a family of four might miraculously squeeze in here at the end of the day. A tent around the back of their apiary proves to be the answer. The caravan is used throughout the summer months to maximise the Chirănescu's honey yield; their actual home is in the Transylvanian city of Râmnicuvâlcea where they'll return no later than the beginning of October for the start of school, both for the children and their father who is a history teacher.

As we position ourselves around the small plastic picnic table in preparation for supper, Razuan reappears like a magician from inside the caravan clutching a raw carrot. In amongst our laughter, I appreciate the intended sophistication of his vegetable entrée, knowing that precious little food can be carried on the move, especially in such heat. Despite the expansive agriculture around us, food supplies are distant. Only their honey is ready for the taking. As the day's light finally dissipates, cutlery is collected and divided equally if somewhat haphazardly while bowls of boiled potatoes dressed with pieces of tomato are carefully passed to everyone in turn. Boiled eggs in their shells follow next and in the dark it's just about possible to see that with fewer eggs than people it's the parents who take less food regardless of their day's fasting. Nevertheless, the jovial spirit of a young family sharing an improvised meal with a foreign guest has a holiday feeling. Perhaps the sound of insects that are still active also provides a certain reassurance of productivity while we relax into the evening. Although we're surrounded by monoculture, something of the profuseness of the area's sunflowers seems to permeate our optimism. Indeed, having wished one another goodnight, only the dog appears perturbed, barking into the silence of the fields that surround us.

* * *

The next morning I'm able to study more of the mobile apiary's construction when Mihaela enters the corridor behind the hives to remove some honeycomb and delicately place it into a glass jar. The box she opens is in principle no different to a standard hive, but its containment within the caravan is certainly distinct: twenty-four hives in total are arranged in three rows of eight with space above for each to be extended by one or two supers. Although once horse-drawn, one look at the caravan's substantial tyres is enough to suggest a faster, mechanical form of transportation is now used to move these hives from one location to the next. The other mobile apiary I'll see on my travels, kept on display at the Living Bee Museum in Knuellwald, Germany, is a 'retired' trailer from East Germany, which, despite its lack of decoration, is near identical to the Romanian caravan. The museum, which also contains other Soviet memorabilia such as large containers for the mass-collection and storage of honey common within Communist farming practice, would also provide comparative evidence of the broad, complex changes exemplified by Mihaela's use of small jars for today's honey collection.

Tiberiu, who is preparing for term time from a book of seemingly simple pages detailing the complexities of recent European history, conveys his calm disapproval of the political developments that have resulted in the current condition of this landscape. The dusty, parched soil beneath our feet, which is only capable of supporting undemanding crops, carries the accumulative weight of many inequitable decisions. Between 1965 and 1989, Romania endured the impact of severe agricultural industrialisation under Nicolae Ceausescu's Communist dictatorship. Tiberiu and Mihaela remember the state's extreme diktat when whole villages were devastated and rural communities relocated to towering concrete blocks in order to increase agricultural landmass. Counter-intuitively, these measures left the country starving. Despite a wealth of knowledge and experience, farmers had no choice other than to follow instructions from Bucharest, which forced them to grow unsuitable crops without rotation and use huge quantities of artificial fertiliser and synthetic pesticides. Yields plummeted as the soil failed, while export* inexplicably continued: food shortages were crippling. A generation may have passed since the collapse of that regime but for those forced into urban life, who now have no land of their own, it is a genuine response to reinvigorate a strong rural past with this landless farming practice. The spirit of adventure that accompanies this family in their summer work is likely based on the pleasure of being able to do something directly productive in their time away from the city. As Tiberiu and Mihaela would have known hunger all too well as children, independent honey production is likely a satisfying and reassuring form of sustenance.

Beekeepers may now be free to journey once more for their own benefit and profit but the country they travel hasn't miraculously

* employed by Ceausescu to repay debts incurred after accepting credit and technical aid from the West

returned to its once-renowned fertility. Since the revolution, potent agricultural chemicals have continued to be produced and used on what is already heavily-treated soil. Tracts of land extended for collectivised farming – which, when privatised, were notably transferred to those influential within the old state system – have remained large-scale monocultures. Since its 2007 entry into the European Union, Romania's most industrialised crop, the sunflower,[1]* has proven less productive than the equivalent grown elsewhere in the EU: both Bulgaria and France produce large-scale sunflower crops with higher yields from less acreage.[2] It is cheap agricultural labour that keeps Romania's sunflower crops competitive.[3]† In a worrying echo of Ceausescu's times, much of Romania's produce leaves the country. Although 60% of Romania is officially classified as rural with 14.7 million hectares of agricultural land – one of the largest landmasses dedicated to farming in the EU – a stark statistic measures the country's current dependency on imported food at 70%.[4]‡ In Romania, Capitalism has all too easily compounded what Communism started.

Looking at the Chirănescu's caravan within its current landscape, I'm reminded once more of its incongruity. The combination of a traditional migratory practice with industrial farming reflects a clash of cultures inherent to much contemporary agriculture that isn't always as evident as it is here today under a clear sky. Although honeybees on this apiary are collecting abundant forage and pollinating the sunflowers in return, something in this relationship is no longer harmonious. Indeed, it may no longer be possible to see all flowers equally optimistically.

* covering near 740,000 hectares of land

† 30% of Romanians are employed within agricultural work and provide 20% of overall farm labour within the EU.

‡ By 2010, a total of 557,409 tons of exported sunflower seed was valued at €214.8 million, and yet Romania imported 208,284 tons of sunflower seeds worth €109.72 million that same year. Despite a yield that was high enough to secure the total requirement of the internal market, farmers chose to sell their seed abroad, forcing the import of sunflower seeds, which ultimately incurred 27% higher import costs than their export value.

Before I leave, Tiberiu and Mihaela hand me two jars of honey: one distinctively liquid yellow, the other proudly displaying comb that was harvested so very recently. While the strong citrus flavour may be waxen, it carries an unmistakable sweetness I'll savour as a reminder of this family's justifiable pride in maintaining their farming tradition despite the odds. The children, who may no more own nor be owned by this landscape than I, then rush forward with a keepsake from the fields: a young sunflower, plucked from background to foreground, which in its sudden singularity regains some of its promise.

endnotes

one

1 Fleming, N., 'Keepers fear mystery bee illness', *The Telegraph*, 13th April 2007

2 Benjamin, A. & McCallum, B., *A World Without Bees: The mysterious decline of the honeybee and what it means for us*, Guardian Books, London, 2008, pp.104–5

3 Ibid., p.101

4 Neumann, P. & Carreck, N., 'Honeybee colony losses', *Journal of Apicultural Research*, Vol. 49, No. 1, 2010, pp.1–6

5 Rennie, J., White, P.B., Harvey, E.J., 'Isle of Wight Disease in hive bees: The etiology of the disease', *Trans. R. Soc. Edinburgh*, Vol. 52, No. 4, Jan 1921, pp.737–755

6 Bailey, L., 'The Isle of Wight Disease: The origin and significance of the myth', March 1963

7 Benjamin, A. & McCallum, B., *A World Without Bees, op. cit.*, p.216

8 Department of Agriculture and Rural Development (DARD), 'Strategy for the Sustainability of the Honeybee', Belfast, Feb 2011

9 Department for Environment, Food and Rural Affairs, 'Farming Statistics: Final crop areas, yields, livestock populations and agricultural workforce at 1 June 2012', London, Dec 2012, www.gov.uk/government/statistics/farming-statistics-land-use-livestock-populations-and-agricultural-workforce-at-1-june-2012-uk [last accessed: Sept 2014]

10 *Ibid.*

11 DARD, 'Strategy for the Sustainability of the Honeybee', op. cit.

12 *Ibid.*

13 *Ibid.*

14 James Hutton Institute, 2007, 'SCRI report', 2007, www.scri.ac.uk/publications/2007annualreport [last accessed: Oct 2013]

15 James Hutton Institute, 'Scotland Joins North Sea Region Coalition to Boost Berry Industry', 17 February 2010, www.scri.ac.uk/news/climafruit [last accessed: Oct 2013]

16 Natural England, 'Traditional Orchard Project in England', Commissioned Report NECR077, Sheffield, May 2011, foreward & p.44

17 Erskine, J. (producer and director), *Who Killed the Honeybee?*, BBC4, April 2009

18 *Ibid.*

19 *Ibid.*

20 European Crop Protection, 'The Reality of Farming: Putting food on your plate', 2012,
www.ecpa.eu/page/reality-farming [last accessed: Jan 2012]

21 Carson, R., *Silent Spring* (excerpts first published in the New Yorker in June 1962), Penguin Books, London, 2000, p.117

22 *Ibid.*, pp.118–9

23 *Ibid.*, p.119

24 Flannery, T., *Here on Earth: A new beginning*, Allen Lane (Penguin Books), London, 2011, p.163

25 *Ibid.*, pp.163–6

26 Carson, R., *Silent Spring*, op. cit, p.47
(in ref. to: Glynne-Jones, G. D. and Thomas, W.D.E., 1953, 'Experiments on the possible contamination of honey with Schradan', *Annals Appl. Biol*, Vol. 40, 1953, p.546)

27 *Ibid.*, p.46

two

1 Maxim, L. & van der Sluijs, J., 'Seed-dressing systemic insecticides and honeybees', *Late Lessons from Early Warnings*, European Environment Agency, Vol. 2, 2012, Kindle file, Ch. 16.2.1

2 *Ibid.*

3 World Health Organisation, 'Evaluations of the Joint FAO / WHO Expert Committee on Food Additives (JECFA)', TRS 959-JEFCA 72 Report, Rome, 2010,
http://apps.who.int/ipsc/database/evaluations/chemical.aspx?chem ID=1863 [last accessed: June 2013]

4 Maxim, L. & van der Sluijs, J., 'Seed-dressing systemic insecticides and honeybees', *op. cit.*

5 *Ibid.*

6 *Ibid.*, Ch. 16.2.2

7 Pilz, C., 'Comparative efficacy assessment of fungi, nematodes and insecticides to control western corn rootworm larvae in maize', *BioControl*, Vol. 54, No. 5, Oct 2009, p.671

8 Meissle et al., 'Pests, pesticide use and alternative options in European maize production: Current status and future prospects', *Journal of Applied Entomolgy*, Vol. 134, No. 5, June 2010, pp.357–375

9 Spürgin, A., 'Bienenvergiftungen durch gebeizte Maissaat:

Informationsveranstaltungen am 24. und 28. Mai in Freiburg und Offenburg' (Bee poisoning from dressed corn seed: Information sessions on 24th and 28th May in Freiburg and Offenburg), Regierungspräsidium (Regional Governmental Authority), Freiburg, 2008

10 Baden-Württemberg Ministerium für Ernährung und Ländlichen Raum (Baden-Württemberg Ministry of Food and Rural Areas), 'Abschlussbericht Beizung und Bienenschäden' (Final report: seed dressing and bee losses), Stuttgart, 17th December 2008, p.6

11 Trenkle, A., 'Bienenschäden 2008 in Rheintal: Analytik, Ursachen, Konsequenzen' (Bee losses in the Rhine Valley 2008: Analysis, causes, consequences), LTZ, Austenberg, Karlsruhe, 2009, p.8

12 *Ibid.*, pp.8–9

13 *Ibid.*

14 *Ibid.*, p.13

15 *Ibid.*, p.11

16 *Ibid.*, p.15

17 Schmuck, R., 'Bayer CropScience: Der Wirkstoff Clothianidin ist bei Sachgerechter Anwendung sicher für Bienen' (Active compound clothianidin is safe for bees when properly applied), Karlsruhe, 20th June 2008

18 Baden-Württemberg Ministerium für Ernährung und Ländlichen Raum, 'Abschlussbericht Beizung und Bienenschäden', *op. cit.*, p.7

19 Trenkle, A., 'Bienenschäden 2008 in Rheintal: Analytik, Ursachen, Konsequenzen', *op. cit.*, p.11

20 Bundesamt für Verbraucherschutz und Lebensmittelsicherheit, 'Pflanzenschutzmittel Verzeichnis' (Plant Protection Products Directory), 2013,
www.bvl.bund.de/EN/04_PlantProtectionProducts/02_Authorized PlantProtectionProducts/PlantProtectionProducts_Authorized PlantProtectionProducts_node.html [last accessed: June 2013]

21 Bundesamt für Verbraucherschutz und Lebensmittelsicherheit, 'Mesurol flüssig (liquid methiocarb) back in use', 2nd September 2009,
www.bvl.bund.de/EN/08_PresseInfothek_engl/01_Presse_und_ Hintergrundinformationen/2009_02_09_pi_Maissaatgut_Mesurol_ en.html?nn=1414138 [last accessed: Nov 2013]

22 Bayer CropScience, 'Seed Treatment with Poncho: Sowing peace of mind', 2003

23 Agentur für Gesundheit und Ernährungssicherheit (Agency for Health and Food Security), 'The MELISSA Report', 2012,
http://www.dafne.at/dafne_plus_homepage/index.php?section= dafneplus&content=result&come_from=&&search_fields[offer_ number]=100472&search_fields[title_ger]=&search_fields[research

_objective]=&search_fields[beauftragungsjahr]=&searchfields
[antragsteller]=&searchfields[projektleiter]=&project_id=2909
[last accessed: Sept 2014]

24 *Ibid.*

25 *Ibid.*

26 *Ibid.*

27 *Ibid.*

28 *Ibid.*

29 Pistorius, J., Bischoff, G., Heimbach, U., Stähler, M., 'Bee poisoning incidents in Germany in spring 2008 caused by abrasion of active substance from treated seeds during sowing of maize', Hazards of pesticides to bees – 10th International Symposium of the ICP-Bee Protection Group, *Julius-Kühn Archive*, 423, 2009, p.118

30 Alaux et al., 'Interactions between nosema microspores and a neonicotinoid weaken honeybees (*Apis mellifera*)', *Environmental Microbiology*, Vol. 12, No. 3, March 2009, pp.774–782;
Pettis, J.S., Lichtenberg, E.M., Andree, M., Stitzinger, J., Rose, R., 'Crop pollination exposes honeybees to pesticides which alters their susceptibility to the gut pathogen *Nosema ceranae*', *PLoS ONE*, Vol. 8, No. 7, July 2013,
www.plosone.org/article/info%3Adoi%2F10.1371%2Fjournal.pone.0070182 [last accessed: Nov 2013]

31 Whitehorn, P.R., O'Connor, S., Wackers, F.L. & Goulson, D., 'Neonicotinoid pesticide reduces bumble bee colony growth and queen production', *Science*, Vol. 336, No. 6079, April 2012, pp.351–352;
Henry, M., Beguin, M., Requier, F., Rollin, O., Odoux, J.F., Aupinel, P., Aptel, J., Tchamitchian, S. & Decourtye, A., 'A common pesticide decreases foraging success and survival in honeybees', *Science*, Vol. 336, No. 6079, April 2012, pp.348–350

32 European Food Safety Authority, 'Conclusion of Pesticide Peer Review: Conclusion on the peer review of the pesticide risk assessment for bees for the active substance clothianidin', *EFSA Journal 2013*, Vol. 11, No. 4, April 2013, p.37

33 *Ibid.*

34 Directorate-General for Agriculture, 2000, 'Economic Impacts of Genetically Modified Crops on the Agri-Food Sector', European Commission,
http://ec.europa.eu/agriculture/publi/gmo/ch2.htm
[last accessed: June 2013] (in ref to: Inverzon International Inc., 1999);
The Council for Biotechnology Information, 2013, http://whybiotech.ca
[last accessed: June 2013]

35 Syngenta letter to European Commissioner, John Dalli, 8th June 2012

36 Maxim, L. & van der Sluijs, J., 'Seed-dressing systemic insecticides and

honeybees', *op. cit.*, Ch. 16.5

37 Bayer CropScience letter to Commissioner Dalli about 'Intention of the French Minister of Agriculture to suspend a highly effective and innovative seed treatment product and the political debate around it', 12th June 2012

38 *Ibid.*

39 Letter from Owen Patterson, Environment Secretary, DEFRA, to Syngenta, 20th April 2013, www.scribd.com/doc/138461467/Owen-Paterson-s-letter-to-Syngenta-on-insecticides-ban-proposals [last accessed: June 2013]

40 European Food Safety Authority, 'Conclusion of Pesticide Peer Review: Conclusion on the peer review of the pesticide risk assessment for bees for the active substance clothianidin', *op. cit.*, p.14

41 'Bee deaths fuel debate about official secrecy', *Der Standard*, 4th–5th May 2013

42 Völker, M., 'Of Citizens and Bees – Official secrecy and plant protection products: Where policy (also) fails', *Der Standard*, 4th–5th May 2013

43 A post-vote event organised by Greenpeace and Global 2000, Vienna, 15th May 2013

44 European Food Safety Authority, 'Conclusion of Pesticide Peer Review: Conclusion on the peer review of the pesticide risk assessment for bees for the active substance clothianidin', *op. cit.*, p.15

45 *Ibid.*

46 "The combination of high pesticide loads and increased Nosema infection rates in bees that consumed greater quantities of the fungicides chlorothalonil and pyraclostrobin suggest that some fungicides have stronger impacts on bee health than previously thought. Nosema infection was more than twice as likely (relative risk >2) in bees that consumed these fungicides than in bees that did not." See Pettis, J. et. al, 'Crop pollination exposes honey bees to pesticides which alters their susceptibility to the gut pathogen *Nosema ceranae*', *op. cit.*

three

1 Frimston, D. & Smith, D., *Beekeeping and the Law: Swarms and Neighbours*, Bee Books New and Old, Somerset, 1993, p.8

2 Wildman, T., *A Treatise on the Management of Bees*, Cadell, London, 1768. See Wilson, B., *The Hive*, John Murray, 2004, p.223

3 Statistical Office of the Republic of Slovenia, 'Agricultural holdings with the number of honeybee colonies by statistical regions', Slovenia, 2000 and 2010,

http://pxweb.stat.si/pxweb/Dialog/varvalasp?ma=15P111E&ti=&
path=../Database/Agriculture_2010/02–Livestock/03_15P11_stat_
region/&lang=1 [last accessed: May 2014]

4 Ruttner, F., 'Biometrical-statistical Analysis of the Geographic Variability of *Apis mellifera* L.', *Apidologie*, Vol. 9, No. 4, 1978, pp.363–381

5 De La Rúa, P., Jaffé, R., Dall'Olio, R., Muñoz, I., Serrano, J., 'Biodiversity, conservation and current threats to European honeybees', *Apidologie*, Vol. 40, No. 3, May–June 2009, pp.263–284 (with ref. to: Ruttner, F., *Biogeography and Taxonomy of Honeybees*, Springer, Berlin, 1988)

6 *Ibid.*

7 *Ibid.* See Jensen, A. B. et al., 'Varying degrees of *Apis mellifera ligustica* introgression in protected populations of the black honeybee, *Apis mellifera mellifera*, in northwest Europe', *Molecular Ecology*, Vol. 14, No. 1, Jan 2005, pp.93–106

8 *Ibid.*

9 Dall'Olio et al., 'Genetic characterization of Italian honeybees, *Apis mellifera ligustica*, based on microsatellite DNA polymorphisms', *Apidologie*, Vol. 38, No. 2, March–April 2007, pp.207–217

10 Benjamin, A. & McCallum, B., *A World Without Bees, op. cit.*, p.64

11 *Ibid.*, p.65

12 *Ibid.*, p.77

13 Chapman, N.C. et al., 'Population genetics of commercial and feral honeybees in western Australia', *J. Econ. Entomol.*, Vol. 101, No. 2, 2008, pp.272–277

14 Delaney, A. A. et al., 'Genetic characterization of commercial honeybee (*Hymenoptera Apidae*) populations in the United States by using mitochondrial and microsatellite markers', *Ann. Entomol. Soc. Am.*, Vol. 102, No. 4, 2009, pp.666–673

15 De La Rúa et al., 'Biodiversity, conservation and current threats to European honeybees', *op. cit.*, p.274

16 Gregorc, A. & Lokar, V., 'Selection criteria in an apiary of carniolan honey bee (*Apis mellifera carnica*) colonies for queen rearing', *Journal of Central European Agriculture*, Vol. 11, No. 4, 2010, pp.401–408

four

1 Svensson, T., 'Increasing Ground Temperatures at Abisko in Subarctic Sweden', Lund University, Sweden, 2008

2 Swedish Commission on Climate and Vulnerability, 'Sweden Facing Climate Change: Threats and opportunities', Stockholm, 2007, p.81

3 *Ibid.*, p.107

4 *Ibid.*
5 Le Conte, Y., Ellis, M., Ritter, W., 'Varroa mites and honeybee health: Can varroa explain part of the colony losses?', *Apidologie*, Vol. 41, No. 3, May–June 2010, p.353–363
6 Kristiansen, P., 'Beekeeping in Sweden', Swedish Beekeepers Association, *op. cit.*, p.6
7 Fries, I., Imdorf, A., Rosenkranz, P., 'Survival of mite infested (*Varroa destructor*) honeybee (*Apis mellifera*) colonies in a Nordic climate', *Apidologie*, Vol. 37, No. 5, Sept–Oct 2006, pp.564-570
8 *Ibid.*
9 Johnson, R.M., Pollack, H.S., Berenbaum, M.R., 'Synergistic interactions between in-hive miticides in *Apis mellifera*', *J. Econ. Entomol.*, Vol. 102, No. 2, April 2009, pp.474-479
10 Le Conte et al., 'Varroa mites and honeybee health: Can varroa explain part of the colony losses?', *op. cit.*, p.356

five

1 Bogdanov, S., 'Contaminants of bee products', *Apidologie*, Vol. 37, No. 1, Jan–Feb 2006, pp.1–18
2 London Beekeepers Association / Food and Environment Research Agency (FERA), National Bee Unit, 'Greater London beekeeping figures 2008 and 2012', London and York, 2014
3 Viljoen, A. & Bohn, K., *Second Nature Urban Agriculture: Designing productive cities*, Routledge, Oxon, 2014
   See Tomkins, M., 'Bricks and Nectar: Urban beekeeping with specific reference to London as an example', pp.84–91
4 Delong, D., 'Are there too many bees in London?: Comments from Angela Woods, secretary of the London Beekeepers Association', *Romancing the Bee*, 2 July 2012,
   http://romancingthebee.com/2012/07/02/are-there-too-many-bees-in...rom-angela-woods-secretary-of-the-london-beekeepers-association/ [last accessed: Sept 2014]
5 The Food and Environment Agency (FERA), Beebase, 'EU Import Report', 2013,
   https://secure.fera.defra.gov.uk/beebase/public/BeeDiseases/euImportReport.cfm?year=2013; 'EU Import Report', 2012, https://secure.fera.defra.gov.uk/beebase/public/BeeDiseases/euImportReport.cfm?year=2012; 'EU Import Report', 2007, https://secure.fera.defra.gov.uk/beebase/public/BeeDiseases/euImportReport.cfm?year=2007 [last accessed: Sept 2014]

6   The Food and Environment Agency (FERA), Beebase, 'Import Report', 2013,
    https://secure.fera.defra.gov.uk/beebase/public/BeeDiseases/importReport.cfm?year=2013 [last accessed: Sept 2014]

7   'Bad weather hits British honey production', *The Guardian*, 30 Oct 2012,
    www.guardian.co.uk/environment/2012/oct/30/bad-weather-honey-bees?CMP=EMCENVEML1631 [last accessed: Nov 2012]

8   British Beekeepers Association, 'Honey Survey 2012', Kenilworth, Oct 2012; Food and Environment Research Agency (FERA), National Bee Unit, 'South-East Honey Survey 2013', York, Oct 2013

9   Benjamin, A. & McCallum, B., *Bees in the City: the urban beekeepers handbook*, Guardian Books, London, 2012, p.77

10 Smith, C., 'London: Garden City?: Investigating the changing anatomy of London's private gardens and the scale of their loss', London Wildlife Trust / Greenspace Information for Greater London / Greater London Authority, London, 2010

11 The London Wildlife Trust, 'Garden for a Living London', www.wildlondon.org.uk/garden-for-a-living-london
    [last accessed: Sept 2014]

12 Gabuzov, M., 'Helping the honeybee and insect pollinators in urban areas', *Functional Ecology*, Vol. 28, No. 2, April 2014, pp.364-374

13 Dicks, L., 'Insects and Insecticides', UK Parliament Environmental Audit, Nov 2012, www.publications.parliament.uk/pa/cm201213/cmselect/cmenvaud/writev/668/m26.htm [last accessed: Jan 2015]
    See Breeze, T.D., Bailey, A.P., Balcombe, K.G., Potts, S.G., 'Pollination services in the UK: How important are honeybees?', Agriculture, Ecosystems and Environment, Vol. 142, No.s 3–4, 2011, pp.137–143
    See Carrington, D., 'Bee crisis: UK government launches 'urgent' review', *The Guardian*, 28 June 2013,
    www.guardian.co.uk/environment/2013/jun/28/bee-crisis-urgent-review [last accessed: July 2013]

14 Carrington, D., 'Grave threat of pesticides to bees' billion-pound bonanza is now clear', *The Guardian*, 11 April 2012,
    www.theguardian.com/environment/damian-carrington-blog/2012/apr/11/bees-pesticides-decline-colony-collapse
    [last accessed: July 2013]

15 Butler, T., 'Natural Capital' is a bankrupt metaphor, *Earth Island Journal*, Summer 2013,
    www.earthisland.org/journal/index.php/eij/article/natural_capital_is_a_bankrupt_metaphor/ [last accessed: Sept 2014]

16 'Beekeepers march on Downing Street to increase funding', *The Telegraph*, 5 Nov 2008,

www.telegraph.co.uk/news/picturegalleries/uknews
[last accessed: Sept 2014]

17 Goulson, D. & Sparrow, K.R., 'Evidence for competition between honeybees and bumblebees: Effects on bumblebee worker size', *Journal of Insect Conservation*, Vol. 13, No. 2, Feb 2008, pp.177–181; National Research Council, 'Status of Pollinators in North America', National Academies Press, Washington D.C., 2006

18 Carrington, D., 'Grave threat of pesticides to bees' billion-pound bonanza is now clear', *op. cit.*

19 Friends of the Earth, Bee Care campaign poster, London, March 2014

20 Couvillon, M.J., Schürch, R. & Ratnieks, F.L.W., 'Dancing bees communicate a foraging preference for rural lands in high-level Agri-Environmental Schemes', *Current Biology*, Vol. 24, No. 11, June 2014, pp.1212-1215

epilogue: *commercial beekeepers*

1 Kamberi, M. A., 'Country Pasture / Forage Resource Profile', University of Prishtinë, Pristina, 2009
www.fao.org/ag/agp/AGPC/doc/Counprof/kosovo/Kosovo.htm
[last accessed: Oct 2014]

2 ARD-BIOFOR IQC Consortium, 'Kosovo Biodiversity Assessment', May 2003, p.16

epilogue: *migratory beekeepers*

1 Barbu, C. M.., 'The Romanian Agriculture: Between myth and reality', *Oeconomica*, Vol. 2, No. 13, 2011

2 European Commission, 'Agriculture in the European Union and the Member States: Statistical factsheet', 2014
ec.europa.eu/agriculture/statistics/factsheets/index_en.htm
[last accessed: Oct 2014]

3 *Ibid.*

4 Barbu, C. M., 'The Romanian Agriculture: Between myth and reality', *op cit.*

list of illustrations

acknowledgements

This book would not have been possible without all those beekeepers across Europe who willing answered my questions and enthusiastically demonstrated both their skill and hives. Although not all are mentioned directly by name in this book, I hope their collective knowledge is nevertheless evident in my words.

Special thanks, of course, go to those agricultural scientists, beekeepers and cultural project workers featured in the book: Alison Benjamin, Helen Bergqvist, Caroline Birchall and Paul Anthony Campbell, Tiberiu and Mihaela Chirănescu, Edwin Clark, Olivier Darné and Emmanuelle Roule, Aleš Gregorc, Hemma Köglberger, Mike Thurlow, Mikey Tomkins, Armin Trenkle, Angela Woods, Sylejman and Ayni Zogliani

The wealth of information I've gained from European bee, beekeeping and Natural History museums has also been invaluable. Of particular note are: the Bienenkunden Museum, Münstertal, Germany; the Bienenmuseum, Orth, Austria; the Cebelarski Muzej, Radovljica, Slovenia; the Living Bee Museum, Knuellwald Germany; the Muséum National d'Histoire Naturelle, Paris, France; the Naturalhistorisches Museum, Vienna, Austria; the Openluchtmuseum, Arnhem, Netherlands; and the Traditional Beekeeping Museum, Stripeikiai, Lithuania.

I would also like to sincerely thank: Christopher Thomson for his fervent encouragement and persistent attention to editorial detail; Caroline Woodley and Kate Chandler for their time and critical input in the final stages of editing; Hemma Köglberger, once again, for her willingness to read and correct the science in part one; Krystian Jones for helping to keep the writing going practically; Peter Dukes for rearranging my lecturing schedule to accommodate initial research; Vinçenc Palushaj for his insights about Kosovo; and Richard Clark, Michael Eder and Johanna Gerhalter, Frank Eurisch and Lena Trenkle, and Ramon Rizahi for their generous introductions.

Finally, thanks go to my extended Bowen–Crow–Danter–Johnson–Teal–Thomson–Walters–Waring family and to all friends, especially those as close as family in Dordolla, Vienna and London.

about the author

Sarah Waring lives and works in the UK and Italy. She studied Fine Art Photography at the Royal College of Art, lectured at the University of Westminster and University of the Arts and worked as a writer and media publishing editor in London. She has travelled extensively throughout rural Europe where her interests in ecology and agriculture have been brought to life especially via hands-on experience in Austria, Italy, Sweden and Wales.

Lightning Source UK Ltd.
Milton Keynes UK
UKOW07f2350090215

245981UK00001B/5/P